The Flavor of Life

By Fr. Giovanni Cucci, S.J.

Edited and translated by Fr. Wafik Nasry, S.J.

CONTENTS

Introduction

Usually one thinks of religious experiences as if they contain a range of information about some more or less important problems of life. Yet if one searches the Gospels looking for clear and distinct answers to the big questions of life: such as the problems of evil and injustice, the fate of those who are wicked, an accurate description of what happens when we die etc., one would be disappointed (recalling Descartes). On all these topics, there is a surprising lack of information, ideas or reasoning.

Instead of facts and reasoning, the Gospels pay great attention to the feelings experienced when facing specific situations. Think of the joy of the Magi when observing the star that shows them the way, the sadness of the rich young man upon hearing the proposal to leave everything and follow the Lord, or the fear of Pilate when hearing the charge that Jesus made Himself Son of God. The disciples of Emmaus, recalling the encounter they had with the Risen LORD and reflecting on the event, acknowledge that while they did not recognize Him with their eyes they were particularly affected by the emotional resonance that His words had aroused in their hearts. It is significant to note that the evangelist, in his account, has preferred to record these inner resonances rather than the educative content of the conversation addressed to the two disciples by Jesus, which must have been quite dense, documented and exhaustive (Cfr. Lk 24: 27-32).

These inner movements, these sentiments mentioned above with precise details are confirmed when confronted with life. As narrated in the pages of the Gospel, these sentiments can be found in the events of life that characterize our existence. In these events, whether they are big or small, the criterion of clarity and distinction does not seem to be of great help. Few things are evaluated on the basis of careful reasoning. More frequently, we make our decisions based on other criteria, relational and affective: a passion for a certain cultural argument, the choice of a university major or a state of life such as marriage, the involvement in a new experience, or any initiative of which we know little or nothing. In these situations, one cannot know exactly how things will occur and/or develop and yet one is called to decide.

The available facts, whether they are few or many, do not take away the uncertainty that characterizes the most important events of life; for this reason, one must first know what one is seeking. In the Gospels, Jesus gives paramount importance to the questions, to the point that they often seem to have greater value than the answers. Jesus did not respond to all the questions posed to Him. Sometimes, He calls the speaker to clarify the question or He answers the question with another question, moving the level of discourse to a more personal level, asking us to engage in order to access the answer. In most cases, Jesus seems to show a particular reluctance towards the so-called "speculative issues" (such as those that were mentioned at the beginning), perhaps because the discussions leave the other person exactly at the same starting point, confirming him in his positions. Considered from this perspective, the outcome of the often-heated debates Jesus had with the Scribes and Pharisees on many different issues, is quite eloquent.

Another particular teaching of the Gospel is that even the extraordinary events in themselves, such as miracles, seem incapable of eliciting faith in God. They are rather presented as ambivalent signs, which challenge the interlocutor, inviting him to take a stand. They can only be helpful in a broader sense, characterized in an essentially emotional context: the docility of the heart, the willingness to listen (which in Hebrew is synonymous with obedience) and the desire to find and fulfill the will of God. These are terms which, unlike the diatribes, set in motion, and invite one to take a journey: "come and see," "seek and you will find," "go and do the same," "come, follow me." The Magi in the second chapter of

Matthew, on one hand, seem totally unprepared either intellectually or in terms of information. They do not know the Scriptures, the language or the local customs. They are naïve and we see them committing tactical and evaluative errors. They ask the help of Herod, a man constantly haunted by the thoughts of possible conspiracies to steal his power. On the other hand, one finds that the most essential element present in them is their *desire* to find the Lord. For this reason, they are presented as characters in motion. The willingness to undertake a journey is the basic element for an experience of God. Lack of knowledge, inability, errors of judgment, can all be overcome when one listens to one's desire.

How can one tell if a desire is just? The indication comes, again, from the sentiments: "They were *overjoyed* at seeing the star" (Mt 2: 10). The word used, translated as "overjoyed," is a term that occurs in the Gospel in only one other place in a situation which has a significant resemblance to the Magi's search:

> [44] The kingdom of heaven is like a treasure buried in a field, which a person finds and hides again, and *out of joy* goes and sells all that he has and buys that field. [45] Again, the kingdom of heaven is like a merchant searching for fine pearls. [46] When he finds a pearl of great price, he goes and sells all that he has and buys it. (Mt 13: 44-46)

The evangelist presents both events with a particular kind of joy, using a precise Greek word (χάράς) which occurs only in these two passages. The Evangelist wishes to indicate a type of joy that no

4

human reality could ever give. It is a joy so precious that it is worth any sacrifice: it is the joy of those who have found the Lord. Even the description of the modality of the encounter is significant: the wise men *see* the baby and *worship* the Lord. The encounter with God always passes through signs able to speak to the hearts of those who seek, helping them clarify and recognize that they have finally found Him.

This Gospel passage tells the reader that one can find the Lord, following the three "*S*" characterizing the search of the Magi: *Star*, *Scripture*, and *Sentiment*. These are three signs that can be read within a story, a narrative, which in turn help one to read the book of one's life, an equally valuable book. Unfortunately, for many people, this book remains closed or is read too late, before one dies. Yet the Gospels seem to tell us that it is precisely in this book, one's life, the signs of the presence of God are to be found.

In the following pages, we have tried to identify these three "*S*" in a narrative context of existence. In this narrative context, self-knowledge is confronted with the knowledge of God; we will do this by presenting the experience of a man who lived the great turning point of his existence thanks to the casual reading of a book. This reading, with time, helped him to understand himself more deeply and to recognize the style of God in his life, bringing to light what was present but dormant, hidden, and perhaps forgotten.

Is it right to speak in general terms of the experience of God and self-knowledge by resorting to a special experience? I believe it is, for several reasons. First of all, it is the very *Word of God* Who presented Himself this way, narrating an experience, the experience of a particular people, with their language, culture, mentality, traditions, sensitivities and history. Yet what happened in Israel is paradigmatic, capable of speaking to the experience of all peoples and cultures, as if to say that this story helps us all to recognize the manifestation of God in history:

> 2 Remember how for these forty years the LORD, your God, has directed all your journeying in the wilderness, so as to test you by affliction, to know what was in your heart: to keep his commandments, or not. 3 He therefore let you be afflicted with hunger, and then fed you with manna, a food unknown to you and your ancestors, so you might know that it is not by bread alone that people live, but by all that comes forth from the mouth of the LORD. 4 The clothing did not fall from you in tatters, nor did your feet swell these forty years. 5 So you must know in your heart that, even as a man disciplines his son, so the LORD, your God, disciplines you. (Dt 8: 2-5)

It is a schooling, recognized within a story, *remembering*, a sacred act, taken from the philosophical reflection, which identifies hermeneutics, interpretation, an essential characteristic of man, to know each other remembering, recounting and listening to others.

The presentation of this experience will be divided into three fundamental moments which are also the three chapters of this book: the desire as an inner place where one can recognize the presence of God and some possible criteria for its reading and interpretation (Chapter I); the spatiotemporal characteristics of the human experience of God, expressed by his corporeality, as a place of decision, and the realization of the desire (Chapter II); the creative imagination as a transforming response, a moment of confirming the decision taken, which in turn presents new possible directions to the narrative of the experience (Chapter III). In these moments, the individual has the impression of being introduced, albeit in a gentle and non-binding manner, although larger than oneself, unknown, but strangely responds to what one was seeking all along.

In these pages, I have therefore tried to present some signs, characteristic of the human experience, signs which in turn can be identified according to the religious experience: feelings, relationships, desires, storytelling, imagination, and symbol. The exploration can in turn become a fruitful point of an encounter between the believer and the unbeliever, for these sentiments are, after all, located in the heart of every man. Rather than whether to adhere to God or not, the question becomes, above all, *to what God / god* one intends to give or hold one's trust? And what consequences may all this have on one's existence and self-knowledge? It is therefore indispensable to read the signs, signs that express the essentially religious experience in the bodily condition. The excellent biblical way to meet God in the *Incarnation* is not a coincidence: returning to oneself, one can recognize the presence of mystery in history.

The journey is certainly not an easy one, but it is unquestionably captivating, and what is at stake is well beyond the narrow path of these pages. It is the truth about ourselves: to learn to recognize what we really want from our life and to be willing to pay the price.

CHAPTER I: LISTENING, DESIRE AND NARATIVE

The Experience of God

In one's life, one notes certain difficult activities, tiring and unpleasant, yet they can bring about peace and consolation once undertaken. Other activities, while beautiful and attractive, can be boring and eventually leave the heart empty. Still others can be ignited with high ideals and lofty intentions which in fact one never implements. Why does this happen?

These simple examples from the ordinary experiences in life manifest an element seemingly capricious and unpredictable yet powerful, namely the world of the *affections*. This is the first element chosen to present the religious experience. The examples described above are not only different in affective resonances but also *a possible way of life*, a story that springs up and unexpectedly opens a world larger than oneself, surprising and non-programmable.

This is the experience of a famous saint of the sixteenth century, Ignatius of Loyola. He learns to recognize the presence and style of God first while reflecting on his own feelings, noting significant elements. He is in his home, recovering from a wound received at the Battle of Pamplona. To drive away boredom, he wishes to immerse himself in some exciting reading, namely the tales of chivalry. The desired stories are not on hand, and he only finds *The Life of Jesus* and *The Lives of the Saints*. Ignatius reluctantly accepts these books, and yet it is precisely these books that show him a new way of life. "Reading the life of our LORD and of the saints, he paused to think and reflect to himself, 'What if I do what St. Francis or St. Dominic did?'" Coupled with these reflections, he also entertained other thoughts, borne from his previous life: great battles, conquests of new cities for the king, the admiration of a beautiful and noble lady... Ignatius seems to be faced with two alternative worlds that succeed one another in his imagination, apparently equidistant. Yet, as he stops to examine them, he begins to identify some peculiar characteristics:

> There was, however, a difference: thinking about the things of the world, he felt very happy, *but when, because of fatigue, he abandoned the though, he felt empty and disappointed.*

Instead, [when he thought of going] to Jerusalem barefoot, eating only herbs, practicing all the known rigors of the saints, *the thoughts consoled him when he stopped, and even after putting them aside he remained satisfied and joyful.* (S. Ignazio di Loyola, *Autobiografia* n. 8, TEA, Milano 1992, p. 40; emphasis added)

Ignatius receives his first fundamental experience of God while listening to the emotional resonances that arise from an ordinary experience: reading. He notes in particular a strange alteration, namely that the thoughts of the world are easily assimilated, but they do not last and eventually leave him empty, with a bitter taste. The thoughts of God, on the other hand, enter with some difficulty; it takes a real inner battle to accommodate them, but once they enter, they create a profound and lasting peace that stimulates and puts in motion the formulation of new projects. Above all, they make what comes to mind easy and practical, although arduous. One reads, "He reflected over many initiatives that were good, always proposing to himself difficult and great enterprises; and while he reflected on them, he seemed to find within himself the energy to actualize them with ease." From this, a second important characteristic is found, namely the point of the emotional culmination of a thought as a possible assessment criterion: a beautiful and desirable, but difficult enterprise, suddenly becomes easy to implement and captures the heart, bringing joy in and contentment with life.

11

An important element of the spiritual life is thus given by the *emotional response* elicited by an experience, rather than by the alleged revelation of theological and doctrinal content or new truths. This is a dimension very present in the *Bible*. A decision made for God, even when it requires a high cost, is always accompanied by the joy of having found a good of inestimable value, as in the famous parable in the Gospel of Matthew (13: 44).

A lasting feeling of peace is typical of profound religious experiences. It is a sentiment capable of penetrating the very depths of one's inner self, spontaneously unifying the heart and the mind, regardless of one's age, social status, or level of education. Often such an experience radically changes one's life. The same emotional response is found in the story of the famous convert, Edith Stein, assistant to the professor of Phenomenology, E. Husserl, at Göttingen. She describes her new state of being in terms of peace and vitality, overflowing from a mysterious but present reality:

> There is a state of rest in God, a full suspension of all the activities of the mind, in which you can no longer draw plans or make decisions, nor do anything, but in which, the future is abandoned to the divine will, an abandonment to one's destiny. This vital inflow seems to spring from an asset and a strength that is not mine and which, without inflecting any violence in me, becomes active in me. The only prerequisite to such a spiritual rebirth seems to be that passive capacity of reception that is located at the most

profound structure of the person (E. Stein, *Psicologia e scienze dello spirito*, Città Nuova, Roma 1996, pp. 115-116).

In these experiences *the letting-be* prevails rather than the *should be*. These experiences are not an effort or a pure act of will, but the encounter with an unforeseen reality that manifests itself in a most unexpected manner and at most unexpected times. This sense of docility, of abandonment, is experienced and lived out as a surrender to an initiative not decided or wanted, but a ceasing of resistance, as in the experience described by the prophet Jeremiah:

> 7 You seduced me, LORD, and I let myself be seduced; you were too strong for me, and you prevailed. All day long I am an object of laughter; everyone mocks me. 8 Whenever I speak, I must cry out, violence and outrage I proclaim; the word of the LORD has brought me reproach and derision all day long. 9 I say I will not mention Him, I will no longer speak in His name. But then it is as if fire is burning in my heart, imprisoned in my bones; I grow weary holding back, I cannot! (Jer 20: 7-9).

It is an experience that shows a discreet but profound transformation at an emotional and interior level.

Is the Experience of God a Projection?

In the various situations encountered thus far, one finds a common element in the conversion stories, a recurring feature that unites the accounts: the person does not decide to convert but is captured and transported to another world. This experience often comes *unexpectedly*, as noted by the experience of Ignatius: a broken leg, lack of chivalry books, the apparently advantageous presence of other types of books. As in the parable, already mentioned, with regard to the treasure in the field, the kingdom of God arises when one least expects it; one "trips over it." The vital element is to be ready to recognize it.

This unpredictability of the experience makes it very questionable to accept the interpretation of a relationship with God in terms of a simple *projection*, to suggest a psychological term. As if faith in God merely expresses a strong need for reassurance that is transformed and *projected* to an external figure as a reference point. The episodes narrated in the Gospel demonstrate a very different situation. The LORD makes Himself present in the most unexpected, and even awkward, moments. Think of the episode of the calling of Peter. Peter is completely busy rearranging the nets, tired and anxious after a night spent in a futile attempt to catch something (Lk 5: 5). The circumstances are even more difficult for Matthew, who is caught by the call of Jesus, while he is in front of the money, "sitting at the tax office" (Mt 9: 9).

This character of unpredictability, proper to the experience of God which is neither decided nor planned, is confirmed by the phenomenon known as *aridity*, crisis or dark night, which is a typical component of the spiritual life. Aridity reconfirms the strange feature of the spiritual life: when one looks for God, God seems not to be found, in direct contrast to projections of any kind. The experience of God occurs in the most *unexpected* times and situations. Aridity and darkness are other constants that emerge from the experience of various different saints. Ignatius, Peter, John of the Cross and Edith Stein have all encountered this condition, being face to face with the unpredictability of the *Totally Other*, and, like affective personal relationships, these experiences cannot be planned.

God cannot be confined in a dynamic of projection. He casts into crisis the attempts to manage and take possession of the sacred. The experience that John of the Cross calls *the dark night* is the description of the meeting with the amazing Elusive Mystery. Unlike a *projection*, it is not under one's control. It appears in the most unexpected moments and ways. When the Mystery presents Himself, He requires, as Stein recognized, one thing only, namely *docility* to welcome Him:

> God, says John of the Cross, is often absent when we seek Him and present when we do not seek Him, or perhaps when we do not want Him to even be present. This frustrating experience of the LORD is the best proof that He is not just a figment of our imagination: if it were, I could make it appear or disappear according to my will (TH. GREEN, *Quando il pozzo si prosciuga*, CVX, Roma 1991, p. 105).

The time of trial, of crisis, in the literal sense of the original Greek, means "judgment." It is an invitation to clarify the authenticity of one's motives and what one is really seeking. On the other hand, as we shall see, these circumstances, when they are recognized and included in the more general context of one's ordinary life, can establish and confirm a vital teaching.

Another characteristic sign of an authentic religious experience is given by *the ability to relate*, the knowing of how to differentiate and recognize the differences between self and the other without aiming at an unreal and dangerous reduction of the other, but rather gaining a realistic knowledge of the other in his qualities, limits, temperament and tastes. The relationship with God in the *Bible* always passes through a mediation; it is never an isolated illumination. One cannot know God without knowing oneself and the other. Plunging into self-knowledge helps one recognize the voice and the presence of God. At the foundation of the biblical interdiction to have no images of God, there is the assumption that the only appropriate image of God is man, created in His image and likeness. The face of the other, asserts the philosopher Lévinas, refers us to the truth, often unknown to us, and in this regard expresses the possible authenticity of our relationship with God. It is a truth confirmed also in the psychological realm, as Rizzuto reminds us:

> I have had patients who were practicing believers and others non-believers. Working with them has taught me that to help them reconsider and change their relationship with the divine it is necessary to speak of religion and the relationship with God in the context of their significant relationships. Awareness of their involvement with others, particularly with parents and with significant adults, allows

them to grasp the connections between these experiences and their form of relationship with God. (A. Rizzuto, *La nascita del Dio vivente*, Borla, Roma 2007, p. 5)

Affections and relationships are key elements for a representation of God that respects the complexity and the mystery, based on trust and reverence. However, they, like any human faculty, ought to be educated and integrated as they may be a source of glare and distortion. Think, for example, of the role expectations can play in a significant decision, or for the assessment and the memory of an experience. Expectations, especially if unconscious, often threaten to charge the situation, the people, the events, with meaning and importance that have little to do with their actual reality.

A little exercise can demonstrate how emotions and affections "filter" an evaluation; this is an experiment usually performed with teenagers. Presented with the explanation that due to a worldwide catastrophe all the Gospels in the world were destroyed, the teens are invited to rewrite a Gospel so that it can be passed on to future generations. What is truly interesting is the unconscious *selection* the teens make when writing the Gospel text: the figure of Jesus is, almost always, presented as He preaches, enchants the crowds, performs wonders and miracles and challenges the ruling priestly class. Much less present, in their portrayal, but equally essential are the emotionally "uncomfortable" aspects as the announcement of the Cross, the exhortation to deny themselves, the detachment to material goods, the call to leave everything for the Kingdom. Equally absent is the Passion of Jesus, who is rejected and ridiculed, who dies alone and abandoned. Emotions tend to select, transform and/or reject values heard and proclaimed countless times. Clarifying this point also helps to elucidate a fairly widespread misconception about religious experiences, namely the illusion that with them one is able to achieve perfect serenity, seeking God in the prodigious and the spectacular, eliminating negative feelings, mood and situations (aggression, sadness, crisis, failure), avoiding the effort to know and live with one's own weaknesses.

The *Bible*, speaking of the experience of God, recognizes the need for an integration of feelings, knowledge and will, unified by what the *Bible* calls *the heart*, understood as the center of man's assessment and decision. To enable this integration, it is essential to analyze several fundamental human and spiritual capacities: a strong and deep *desire*; tolerance towards *frustration*, especially when confronted with an unpleasant or ungratifying situation; the ability to live the *renunciation* to achieve a greater good; the motivations and the underlying *values*.

The Truth of Desire: the Narrative Dimension of the Experience of Faith

This is the element at the foundation of the profound change in the life of St. Ignatius, the focal point of his encounter with God: "Desiring to imitate the saints, he sought nothing else save the hope, that with the grace of God, he will do as well as they had done." (S. Ignazio di Loyola, *Autobiografia* n. 9, cit., p. 41)

The desire may be considered the "fulcrum" that combines cognition, affection and will, all the elements present in the act of a decision. This is the reason why, a desire involves the whole person because, although closely related to affection, at its base there is also an evaluative component. Knowing and adequately realizing a desire is crucial because it means that one knows what one wants from one's life and is willing to face the risks, sacrifices and obstacles to achieve it.

The word "desire" comes from a Latin word, *de-sidus*, which literally means "the absence of the star." A desire spontaneously evokes the awareness of "a lack of something" and "a dynamic tension" to achieve the good corresponding to it. This means that the taste for accomplishing something constitutes only one aspect of the desire. The other equally important aspect is given by the limits, as we shall see, of what constitutes the corporality intended as boundaries. Together they are the threshold of reality.

The world of desires leads the individual to live according to a continuous expansion and reveals to the individual one's infinite potential. At one's birth a person may indeed learn any language, implement any project; everything seems equally placed before the range of possibilities. One could become an entrepreneur, a teacher, an explorer, a pilot, an athlete, a monk ... The desire opens the door to ten or to a thousand other possible desires. The desire knows not the words, "final end." Rather, it seems to grow over time: reading a book recalls countless other literature, knowing a person places one in relation with other persons. Any experience stimulates new and different possibilities.

This sense of unfinished infinity, proper to a spiritual being, can be further recognized considering the imaginative and fantastic qualities present in the desire. Through thinking, without moving from one's room, one can find oneself in another place, think of different people, converse about the most beautiful things without the trouble of having to explain, follow a logical thread, or the difficulty of being cautious, without need for clarifications. The desire, *continuously expanding*, when it is cultivated by the imagination, it rewards the individual with a certain sense of omnipotence, never exhausting the possibilities.

The desire provides the ability to make choices that remain unexplained on the pure basis of education received, public opinion or social pressure, as if drawing from an irreducible personal element of truth. The English writer, Chesterton, in his book *Heretics*, makes an interesting observation in this regard "The spirit of the time is made up of those who are indifferent to it, but they know what they want."

Can one "rank" one's desires? Can one establish criteria for recognizing their validity and their truth, other than their irresistible strength? The desire, due to its potent ability to move one to action, can also constitute a danger, with tragic consequences. Ignatius himself experienced the fact, at his expense, when he felt a strong desire to kill a Moor after a heated discussion on matters of faith. (cfr. S. IGNAZIO DI LOYOLA, *Autobiografia* nn. 15-16, cit., pp. 45-46)

The simple sentiment in itself, therefore, even if strong and invasive, is not synonymous with truth. Thus, *one must learn to read the desire*, recognizing some possible interpretative criteria, and to do this one needs to place a certain distance from what one has experienced. It is similar to when one wishes to observe a whole city or a region; one can do so only from above. To understand what happened, what one is seeking, it is appropriate, as is done with a book, to stop and re-read carefully and slowly, noting what touches the heart.

In addition to deep peace and inner joy, an important criterion, in the order of the possible truth of a desire, and at the same time characteristic of the experience of God, is its *durability*. When Ignatius decided to put his experience in writing, 35 years had already passed, yet the thought of Jerusalem still captured and moved him deeply.

Ignatius realizes that God makes Himself known in time, in concrete historical circumstances; God is not to be sought in some kind of an intangible world but in the heart of the human experience. The good is always concrete and is linked to the precise situation in which one is living:

> According to Ignatius, it is not possible to say in general what is best for people because there is no "greater good" in the absolute, but the good is always historical, relative to individual situations, which comes in the ever changing and different aspects [of one's life]. (M. Perniola, *Del sentire cattolico*, Il Mulino, Bologna 2001, p. 100)

Hence the importance of putting order to one's thoughts and desires by placing them within a story, a narrative, recognizing a first and a second, a before and after and a possible end point. In this way one can elaborate a more general design, one can contextualize the desire beyond the possible accidental and unforeseen randomness of single episodes. Ignatius himself experienced this randomness (the lack of books of chivalry in the house, the alternation of opposite feelings to the readings, the inability to embark for Jerusalem...), but with time, he recognized that these details had a continuity and showed a path that united them, a definite end point, which also corresponded to an inner feeling of peace, joy, and inner unity. Hence, he learned to interpret what moved in his heart.

Time is, indeed, a valuable and objective parameter, in the sense that escapes the arbitrariness of the individual. Time helps us understand the inner feeling, recognize the matter as an objective fact: the durability and permanence of the desire, and the success of a possible realization that does not depend on us. The experience of the biblical God is always linked to a temporal dimension: God is the LORD of time; He is presented as "the One who is and who was and who is to come" (Rev 1: 8). It is not a coincidence that the greatest gift that Israel receives, the height of the Torah and the condition of its fulfillment, is a day, the Sabbath. The Sabbath makes possible the observance of the commandments. As noted by the Jewish philosopher Heschel (*Il sabato*, Garzanti, Milano 1999, pp. 111-112), in the Torah God asks His people not to aspire to the things of space, teaching them to desire the reality of time. For this, He gives them a day, Saturday, which bears the first fruits in anticipation of eternal life. It is the only day of creation of which it does not say, as for every other day, "Evening came, and morning followed" (cfr. Gen. 2:3-4a). Not knowing a sunset, Saturday comes as the culmination of creation, expressed by two fundamental actions: the blessing and the Creator's rest.

Time recalls the liturgical dimension of life with God, which is deepened in the celebration, becoming a time of the *re-reading of the week*. Remembering the Sabbath, man learns to stop and review the previous days, thereby appropriating them. It is then that man can become aware of what he has lived. In this way, the previous days become truly "his," part of his life. In this way, he can realize a significant psychological formula, "Be present to the present moment," knowing oneself to be alive and recognizing what one is accomplishing.

When man ignores this "liturgical dimension," he becomes alienated, lost in the things he does, without being able to taste them, becoming a slave. It is the inherent risk of the technological society that knows neither rest nor recreation because it has lost the sense of simply being, the sense of the blessing of the Sabbath. Forgetting this relationship with time, with God and with creation, all expressed by the celebration of the seventh day, man no longer finds meaning; he loses his place within creation. Not surprisingly, the first question that God addresses to the sinful man is not: "What did you do?" But rather, "Where are you?" Within the liturgy, a time volunteered and celebrated, man is reconciled with God and with creation; there, he finds himself.

The dimension of time, therefore, tells us much about the truth and the consistency of thought and desire. The philosopher Hegel noted that to assess the actual depth of a thinker one needs to put two centuries between him and us. The progress of time shows his depth and the speculative value of his thought. A similar argument can be applied to the desires that surge in the heart, soon they are confronted with difficulties, trials, objections, and contingencies of various kinds. A genuine desire, capable of touching the depth of one's being brings peace, uniting thought, affection, understanding and will. It does not pass away with the passage of time. Rather, as in the parable of the mustard seed (Mk 4: 31-32), it grows more and more. Difficulties and failures usually do not stifle a deep desire. On the contrary, they strengthen the desire even more. It is similar to what ensues when one is thirsty; if one does not drink, the desire to drink is not dropped; rather, it is intensified. In fact, at one-point the desire to drink occupies the whole of one's thoughts and projects. Stability is a good sign for the desire, especially when one is aptly disposed to seek and do the will of God, the LORD of time.

The deepest desires seem to show the same characteristics in intelligent people, namely humility and simplicity. The deepest desires discreetly aim at small and modest things; yet they open up wide horizons. In this regard, for St. Ignatius, crucial help comes from the constant practice of the *examination of conscience*, a time when one stops to reread the day just lived according to a particular point of view. The examination of conscience, made according to certain rules, among other benefits, helps the individual recognize the profound desires of one's heart, while developing one's inner freedom.

Learning how to read one's day from the perspective of openness and attentive listening protects one from making of one's subjectivity the criterion of choice. Often times, certain events, along with an unexpected circumstance, solidify a previous resolution and invite one to adjust it, bringing it to maturity. The operating thread of a narrative of one's action also allows one to place an event in its broader context and gives it a non-arbitrary meaning, beyond the intentions of its author. The historicity of the experience of God ought not be confused with subjectivism, even if the individual is the seat of this reading; one is called to interpret and recognize what happened. In fact, the ultimate responsibility (in the etymological sense of responsiveness) falls upon the individual alone.

Another important feature of genuine desire, closely linked to the previous one, is that when one decides to adhere to it, strangely the difficulties seem surmountable, and one feels able to face them with strength and generosity. This is one of the most striking elements of the new experience that touched Ignatius:

> He reviewed many initiatives that were good, and always proposed to himself difficult and great enterprises; yet while proposing them, he seemed to find within

> himself the energy to easily implement them. (S. Ignazio di Loyola, *Autobiografia* n. 7, cit., p. 39)

The durability of a desire in the face of difficulties as an indication of its truth and origin is an established teaching of spiritual writers. St. Augustine speaks of the desire as a spiritual vessel, the more one devotes oneself to it, the more the desire grows, expands, and the more God can manifest His generosity, filling the individual with His gifts. St. Gregory the Great interprets the many attempts of Mary Magdalene seeking the LORD at the tomb in the same way. These attempts manifest the dynamic characteristic of the spiritual desire that grows and becomes stronger when one tries to implement it, discovering a capacity for overcoming trials and difficulties:

> She sought a first time, but did not find; she persevered in trying, and was given to find. The holy desires grow with time. If they fade in the waiting, it is a sign that they were not true desires. (S. Gregorio Magno, *Omelie sui Vangeli*, II, XXV, 2, in *Opere di Gregorio Magno*, Città Nuova, Roma 1994, vol. II, p. 313)

An exemplar of this point of view is the life of Saint Teresa of Avila. In the face of the mission Jesus communicates to her, namely the reform of Carmel, she meets opposition and refusal. Yet, she serenely obeys the external authorities, even though she, in her own estimation, sees the authority as incapable of evaluating what is happening. Her inner freedom, based upon full confidence in God, allows her to face the obstacles in a peaceful way, manifesting the same peace and serenity of Jesus, who always invites her to *obey without fear*. The project will be achieved in His own time. When her confessors argue that her alleged apparitions are the work of the devil, Teresa is willing to freely put aside everything, limiting herself to observe that the truth would be clear with the passing of the time, certainly not depending on her:

> The LORD told me not to worry, and that I did well to obey, and that soon the truth would be manifest [...]. The LORD not only did not dispense me of obedience, but strongly recommended it, and at the same time assured me that it was Him. (S. Teresa di Gesù, *Vita* 29, 6.7, in Id., *Opere*, Postulazione Generale O.C.D., Roma 1981, pp. 282-283)

Similarly, Ignatius presents the text of *The Spiritual Exercises*, the result of years of work and spiritual experiences, to the theologians of the Inquisition who interrogate him about them, ready to destroy them if they find errors and/or inaccuracies. (cfr. S. Ignazio di Loyola, *Autobiografia* n. 68, cit., pp. 92-93)

Progress in virtue is another accurate criterion for recognizing the deep desire. Teresa of Avila answered those who defined her experiences as the fruit of imagination or diabolic temptation in such terms. She wrote,

> For me, it was impossible to believe that the devil had been the author [of the experience], for he could have used them in an attempt to displace and bring me to hell. Weeding out my vices and filling me with

masculine courage and other virtues is an
expedient so contrary to his own interests.
(S. Teresa di Gesù, *Vita* 28, 13, in Id., *Opere*,
cit., p. 276; trans. slightly modified)

The desire to reform one's life and
strengthening one towards what is good is a common
consequence of a genuine desire, as Ignatius
recognizes while rereading the incident at the origin
of his conversion (cfr. S. Ignazio di Loyola,
Autobiografia n. 9, cit., p. 41). When the desire is good,
it leads to an increased intensity of one's life, and one
notes a higher consistency, fullness, creativity and
initiative in the course of one's day. One experiences
contentment with life, as a result of an unexpected
beauty, which is the distinguishing characteristic of
genuine desire, as in the comments of Peter standing
amazed before the Transfiguration of the Lord. One
would want to remain there simply because "It is
good to be here." Desiring, in this sense, regards
what is beautiful and deserves to be lived to the full.
Classical thought notes a close link between beauty,
truth and goodness. Beauty attracts due to its ability
to communicate what is found at the depth of being.

The authentic desire always presents unity and
profound circularity. It is unifying because, as noted
above, it is capable of engaging feeling and intellect,
affection and will, leaving the person at peace and in
harmony, even in difficult situations. It is circular
because within this dynamic one aspect helps the
other. For example, once one decides to devote an
hour a day to silent adoration, strangely this hour,
rather than taking valuable time away from other
important activities (a typical temptation when one

starts praying!), on the contrary helps the individual to live the remaining hours of the day better. The precise initiative beneficially influences other aspects of one's life, which seem to show no apparent connection to it.

This complex and articulated reading of one's desires is not a mere option, left to the eccentricity of those who have important things to think about, rather it is an essential help to know what one wants from one's life. Many people suffer because they do not know what they really want; they have never made contact with their deep desires. Without sufficient inner clarity one runs the risk of spending one's existence in attempts and maneuvers of various kinds, to finally make one choice while in fact one was seeking another. In this way, the desire is not able to express its truth, and one wastes precious opportunities. Unfortunately, some people undertake important decisions in their lives without being adequately prepared, following the impulse of the moment. It could happen that only after several years, when the fundamental choices have already been made, they are faced with the bitterness of misunderstanding.

Learning to interpret the desire, by inserting it in a more general narrative, helps one recognize possible deviations from the correct path and teaches one how to learn from the lived experience, allowing the individual to interrogate and question. Similar to science and civilization, the spiritual life advances through trial and error; even sin, when it is acknowledged, contains a lesson, and if it is not recognized one risks remaining a prisoner, repeating what has already been done. As observed by the philosopher Santayana, "The man who does not know his own history is doomed to repeat it."

The desire, when educated and contextualized, helps the person bring order into one's life and construct a pacifying unity and circularity which Augustine calls *Ordo amoris*, the order that is born of love and is capable of giving the right value to everything in the light of a profound harmony and balance.

The Ability to Live the Renunciation

The confrontation with time allows one to verify the consistency of desires, manifesting to the individual whether one is really willing to pay the price of their realization. It is often said that difficulties and obstacles are not always unfortunate disasters to be avoided at all costs, but are also moments of truth. They are to be expected and one is to be prepared for them. It is not a coincidence that the next stop on Ignatius' path is marked by a series of very strong trials, on both the affective and transcendent levels. Ignatius quickly realized that the spiritual life is a fight and the enemies to be fought are quite different from what he envisioned. The trials found him displaced and unprepared, almost breaking him. All of which caused him tremendous unexpected suffering, leading him to the brink of suicide (cfr. S. Ignazio di Loyola, *Autobiografia* nn. 20-25, cit., pp. 50-55). At the end of this terrible ordeal, Ignatius acknowledges that in order to win, the grace of God and self-knowledge are equally important.

This time of verification, not lacking in doubts and difficulties, is typical of the spiritual path. What Ignatius experienced is found in many biblical characters, to the point of positing a constant in the experience of God: think of the trials of the patriarch Joseph which lasted 15 years, or Moses and the long, silent apprenticeship that he must fulfill before finally receiving a mission from God at the age of 80, when one no longer thinks of a mission, or Paul's 14 years of trials, sufferings and subsequent disappointments after the mysterious encounter with the LORD at the gate of Damascus.

These different experiences converge in showing the character of "agony" in the Christian life. It is interesting to note how a deep and balanced spirituality *demonstrates* similar characteristics to those of mature affectivity. Emotional maturity, although not the same as the depth of religious experience, has a definite influence on the *quality* of the spiritual life, in particular with regard to the role availability plays for what is in the heart, to make choices, even unpopular ones.

One thinks, for example, about the fundamental capacity one needs in the spiritual experience, namely to live *the renunciation.* The renunciation refers to how an individual can persevere in a choice while not having received the rewards expected, even consciously disregarding them. Ignatius in the face of difficulties does not give up, rather he confirms the decision previously made. This is the reason that in *The Spiritual Exercises* he is careful to encourage that in the time of difficulties, which he calls "spiritual desolation," one never ought to make changes, rather one must reaffirm the original choice made by acting exactly the opposite of what is suggested by the moment of difficulty (S. Ignazio di Loyola, *Esercizi spirituali* nn. 318-319, Edizioni Paoline, Cinisello Balsamo [Mi] 1988, pp. 227-228). This does not mean that one never ought to make changes; what is important is not to do so while one is experiencing a difficulty, when one feels sad and unfulfilled. Once one is experiencing sufficient peace and serenity, features of the detachment mentioned above, one will also recognize the most effective way to make changes if they are needed.

In this instruction, one can see the close relationship between body and spirit: the emotional element and the underlying mood powerfully affect the cognitive processes of evaluation and decision, as we shall see in Chapter Three. Knowing how to *let go* of instant gratification, showing steadfastness in the time of temptation, manifest that the motivation is not solely linked to pleasure, to having everything at once (the dynamic stimulus-response typical of the child) but that one is able to look beyond, to a greater good and greater value. Living the renunciation means faithfulness to the choice made, with stability and ability to persevere.

The dimension of struggle and tension is recognized as important in the human behavioral sciences. In psychology, for example, one speaks more precisely of *optimal frustration*, understood as *the renunciation* of harmful habits in order to achieve more easily the value sought. It is a form of asceticism essential to self-knowledge, for example, in the personal situation of a therapeutic relationship, when the person begins to work on themselves. It is often a painful enterprise, certainly unfulfilling, in which the therapist does not respond to requests to avoid this difficulty, often leaving the fulfillment of the person's needs frustrated. However, it is precisely this very difficult path, faced without fearing it or escaping it, that leads to a deeper contact with oneself. With time one can live better even with problematic areas, leading to a more realistic self-esteem.

The capacity for self-control remains fundamental for one to live the renunciation because it allows the individual to deal with tension both freely and consciously, which is an equally important aspect of the spiritual struggle. The mature person does not lose his peace in the face of tension. He does not call into question the choice he has made. Such a person is able to remain in the situation, showing profound freedom and stability that are not lost in the face of possible conflicts such as the disapproval of others or criticism of thought and/or behavior that is coherent with one's choice of life.

Remaining steadfast in one's choice during difficult times does not mean being rigid, unable to change one's mind or to listen to any criticism; on the contrary, it is the basis for knowing how to accept and appreciate them. Affective education, which is through both choices and sacrifices, increases inner freedom and the ability to question oneself in the face of possible disapproval and objections, and enables one to find a psychological response in the binomial flexibility-rigidity with regard to one's general positions, with the evaluation criteria. It is the ability to know and appreciate people who present convictions, choices and life experiences different from our own. Flexibility as an intellectual attitude, emotional and temperamental in general, certainly requires effort and goes in the opposite direction of spontaneity. Being flexible means to have passed that stage of life summarized by Freud with the term *pleasure principle*, which is contrasted with the *reality principle*. The pleasure principle is not just about openly sexual expressions but addresses also other gratifications, subtler, but no less toxic, related for example to power, to emotional blackmail, to complacency, to an inability to say what one thinks out of fear of losing the approval of others.

These considerations show how spirituality and psychology have an interesting convergence of views: to achieve an objective or a project requires consistency and durability able to overcome an emotion, be it intense but fickle and superficial. Spontaneity alone can become a major obstacle to the ability to make important decisions, which require toil and renunciation:

> Theorizing that inhibits repression is absurd. For the human ego to develop, it has to repress, that is place limits. Repression has the vital function of enabling man to act without dispersion, to concentrate his energies. To have a human existence, man must set limits. (A. Manenti, *Vivere gli ideali. Fra paura e desiderio/1*, EDB, Bologna 1988, p. 211)

Even the experience of faith can be subtly or blatantly animated by the need to receive pleasure and comfort. In such cases, there is a risk of reducing faith to a generic "feel good," a tranquilizer against pain, a kind of "opium" as was recognized by the so-called "masters of suspicion" (Marx, Niche & Freud): a vision in which God tends to disappear to make space for the self and its need for self-realization.

Still another significant criterion to acknowledge, from the human and psychological view, is the emotional maturity of the experience of faith which lies in the ability to appreciate the other's complexity and his experience. It is the ability to know how to consciously understand and adapt to the ways of thinking and feeling different from one's own. It is a recognition of the other's uniqueness, his specific characteristics; even if something is not shared or held in common, it does not affect one's underlying appreciation and esteem for the other.

Empathy, relationship, complexity and flexibility proceed hand in hand with internal freedom, making one able to recognize limits and flaws without fear. In fact, one can only do this with substantial positive self-esteem. Such a one does not feel threatened by the presence of fragility and weakness, expressing a contentment with life that allows one to look beyond oneself.

Steady complaints, conflicts in relationships, sour and pungent answers, deep anxiety, a continuous search for approvals and cheers, and an inability to enjoy the beauty of living all raise difficult questions about the individual's possible emotional maturity (cfr. A. Cencini, *Nell'amore*, EDB, Bologna 1995, p. 90).

Given the conditions pointed out up to now, the tension can become fruitful and make life interesting. It is a difficult journey suffered, but suffered for liberation. At some point, one realizes with amazement that he can live with a need, until then considered indispensable, with more freedom and that the need may in fact be inferior to another.

The Motivation and the Value

Desire is the richest and most complex emotion because, as noted before, it encompasses both an evaluative and cognitive component, namely motivation. Thanks to motivation one can dare make challenging and risky choices, possible in theory to all but implemented effectively only by those who can cope with the renunciation until one's death. In these cases, one recognizes that what is at stake is more valuable than physical life itself; hence, one is acting on the basis of an already proven fullness of life, making one capable of acts which are humanly repugnant. Think of the work among the lepers of Calcutta accomplished by Mother Teresa in the space of a lifetime, or the work among the severely handicapped carried out by Saint Joseph Cottolengo, or the testimony given by people who are able to perform very difficult actions that are hard to understand if not perceived in relation to a motivation which exceeds human logic. In these cases, the total gift of one's life for love of another seems to lie in a horizon of values placed beyond the imagination itself:

> A good novelist could probably invent a character like Father Damien, who lived and died among the lepers of Molokai; but to be Damien one needs a vision of life that would give meaning to a similar life. Another example is Maximilian Kolbe (B. Kiely, *Il bene e la sua valutazione*, Manoscritto 1999, p. 55).

What sustains this vision of life, especially in difficult times, is the capacity to love and to remain in love in the midst of an unpredictable, frustrating, contentious and difficult relationship. This is called self-giving love, for each to know how to love the other, not for the gratification that one can gain, but because it is him or her. Friendship, a loving relationship, highlights the ability to give; it is an expression of freedom and self-control. To reach self-giving, the person must in fact be able to master his emotions and his needs, which would or could lead in other directions; while emotions and needs are always present they do not have to be acted upon. For the beloved, one is able to sacrifice immediate gratification, even at one's own expense.

It is this type of love that can realize affectively strong relationships, such as friendship, marriage, or the choice of celibacy for the Kingdom, expressions of *fidelity* that exceed any immediate infatuation or superficial sympathy. This type of love is not expressed in just a single action, even if it were as extreme as accepting death for an ideal. One could find many examples of people willing to face death for many different reasons. Rather this type of love is persevering in one's choices for years and years, facing the strain and the erosion of time well beyond any enthusiasm or emotional fulfillment. Basic affective experiences such as friendship and love cannot be understood in the context of self-realization. Quite the opposite, friendship reveals its quality precisely in self-sacrifice. Contrary to a view of existence aiming at self-fulfillment and personal pleasure, it is the ability to sacrifice/give oneself, as the *Little Prince* would say, of his "special" red rose.

The decisive factor here is not the need but the *value*, what is valuable in itself, beyond possible emotional gratification. Very difficult cases indeed are seen in the examples referred to above such as Mother Teresa and Maximilian Kolbe. The value understood in this sense unifies mind and heart and becomes the central element of the person and of their life, so much so that it sums up all the other components of their life.

When the *value* does not reach this level of cohesion, it is perceived as a rift in the person. In words he speaks the truth and importance of a principle, but in fact he fails to live it. He is deprived of it because it is lost at the expense of other elements, which are felt by the individual as the effectively central reality. The capacity to renounce, in view of what is deemed spiritually pivotal, becomes a concrete sign of self-control, a testimony of a stable and lasting fidelity as well.

Lonergan affirms that religious choices can be compared to falling in love, an experience not deducible from principles; yet, it changes the way one sees life and invites one to come out of oneself to meet the other.

> Religious conversion consists in being taken by what touches us in an absolute sense. It is falling in love in an other-worldly manner. It is surrendering totally and forever without conditions, restrictions or reservations. (B. Lonergan, *Il metodo in teologia*, Queriniana, Brescia 1975, pp. 256-257)

Value and knowledge

One's path to maturity, emotional and spiritual, is not necessarily related to the cultural and intellectual progress of the person. One who is calm and at peace with oneself is usually less tormented by problems of justification and is content because he has in fact surpassed them. On the other hand, one who experiences an inner discomfort has to constantly deal with these issues, thus acquiring greater expertise with regard to these problems.

Research conducted in this area shows that people who are capable of great commitment and self-donation do not necessarily excel in reasoning skills about the choices to be made. On the other hand, it is equally true that a remarkable intelligence and considerable preparation may not yield an equally high moral and spiritual life:

> It is not necessary to have reached the highest stage of moral reasoning to be able to live as committed people. Exceptional

> and consistent moral commitment also require other qualities or virtues, and not just a developed capacity for moral reasoning. (B. Kiely, *Maturità del ragionamento morale e maturità della vocazione cristiana*, in L. Rulla, ed., *Antropologia della vocazione cristiana. III Aspetti interpersonali*, EDB, Bologna 1997, p. 214)

The last element of decision-making and its consistency with chosen values cannot therefore be identified as part of rational justification. These come at a later time, "after the fact," to better understand the reasons for what has already been implemented. With time, this argumentative and supporting dimension, the reasoning in general, loses importance and they are transformed into a more nuanced, deeper and unified capacity to both know and do the good. It is what medieval authors called the *good habit*, the virtue, the inclination to easily perform a certain type of action, even if objectively unpleasant. In this way, the right action shows itself as natural with the recognized value of reason.

To favor the virtues, intellectual knowledge and critical reasoning of values are not enough. In addition, from the affective perspective, moral and spiritual, *sound traditions and significant educative figures are crucial* because it is through them that the values are internalized, as well understood by Pascal:

> we are habitual but no less spiritual; and here is the instrument with which we are persuaded; it is not only through the demonstration. How few are the things demonstrated! The evidence convinces the spirit alone. The habit makes stronger the

evidence and all more believable.... (B. Pascal, *Pensieri* 470 ed. Chevalier, in Id., *Pensieri, opuscoli, lettere*, Milano, Rusconi, 1978, p. 583)

A mature person, although he may not always have present before him evidence and rational arguments, proves able to persevere in a choice recognized as good. The passage of time, the occurrence of any change to the initial motivation, the absence of loved ones, the change of positions, places, roles, and even physical decay, all these can be dealt with by a deeper and more complex adherence to virtue rather than a more intellectual or emotional path.

Fr. Giovanni Cucci, S.J.

CHAPTER II: THE DECISION, MEDIATION OF THE SOIL

The Body, the Criterion of a Healthy Religiosity

The historical and narrative dimension of the spiritual experience, highlighted in the previous chapter, is linked to a fundamental aspect of human life, namely *one's corporality*. The rooting of one's existence in space and time is a decisive place to recognize the presence of God: one could express this fact, with a well-known theological formula, namely that it is an experience of the *incarnation*. The value recognized by the desire requires a realization in a precise context, which in turn refers to a specific historical tradition and a concrete community. All of this, while presenting problems and difficulties, inconsistencies and possible betrayals of the value, is the only condition for the value's effective execution.

For the most part, the biblical experience of God escapes the spectacle that does not know such experience as a narrative that knows not how to privilege daily life, even in the fundamental events of revelation. This ability, knowing how to enter into one's historical context and cultural environment, is an important sign of maturity of the faith experience. In this respect, one can even recognize a positive and realistic meaning to the term *mediocrity*, a willingness to strive to implement the fundamental desire in the context of ordinary life without surrendering to the defects, obstacles and weaknesses that always accompany one's mundane existence. An experience of reality necessarily passes through limits, an element essentially linked to the body, the only mode of access to the experience of the Absolute available to man.

This theme is well explored by contemporary philosophical reflection. The particularity of one's own point of view, characteristic of corporality, refers simultaneously to the totality of the context, first harvested in the negative, in terms of horizon and background:

> The visible (the body) conveniently placed is carved by the invisible -- The common

> clothing of which all the structures are made
> is the visible, which in turn is not objective of
> itself, but transcendental [...]; seeing is always
> seeing more than what one sees. (M. Merleau-
> Ponty, *Il visibile e l'invisibile*, Bompiani, Milano
> 1969, pp. 216.180)

The awareness of knowing a point of view, while perceiving other possible perspectives, without being able to really know the whole of them (e.g. the perception of the facade of a building implies the other aspects within which we know exist even though we cannot see them) spontaneously manifests that the corporeality and the spirituality of a human being are deeply intertwined. Recognizing the partiality of one's views as a being with a body located in space and time enables one to grasp a larger perspective along with one's own limits. One's perception is confronted with the Totality, the Transcendent, even if one is unable to give "It" an appropriate name because by definition "It" escapes the point of view of the person who scrutinizes "It."

In the perception of the human being resides the ability to transcend oneself, to overcome one's finitude and to recognize a larger horizon; but this can only occur from a precise root, namely one's corporeality. A human being is a point of view of the whole, and one knows that he is unable to exhaust it. Nonetheless, it is exactly this knowledge that allows one to transcend oneself rather than being a prisoner of one's limited perspective. Here lies one's root, essentially dialogical and relational, that enables one to know oneself only by confronting the self with others, in the context of a larger horizon than what one has experienced oneself.

This dialectic perspective, this larger horizon, this totality, is very present in the *Bible*. Think of the final pages of the book of Job in which God is repeatedly asked to give an answer to the problem of the suffering of the righteous. God intervenes, relocating the interlocutor's point of view completely. He shows Job, in a breathtaking rapid series of images, the most diverse creatures, the infinitely large and the infinitely small, the entire horizon of what is, asking each time, "Where were you when I did this?" (cfr. Job 38-41) God responds to Job in a strange way: without stopping at the precise issue that has punctuated the whole debate of the book, God offers a wider and deeper perspective that Job does not know how to grasp. The Almighty thus offers Job a different view of what tormented him. God does not take Job away from the situation but presents him with the possibility of changing his way of thinking.

The body reveals much about the relativity of the human being as well as one's absolute capacity. The same duality used to designate the relationship between one and one's body, the *identical-difference* of oneself, indicates both the beyond and the superabundance. Man is a body but at the same time he is not reduced to mere corporality. Therefore, one can say, "*I am* but also *I have my body.*" There is something that reaches beyond a pure objectification of the body, something which points beyond the body but always starts in the body. (cfr. G. Marcel, *Être et avoir*, Aubier, Paris 1935, p. 12)

All this involves significant consequences for the spiritual life that must respect the mind-body duality. A human being is structurally rooted in the earthly perspective, expressed by one's corporeality. Although one can transcend it, one can never abandon it. Otherwise, one is bewildered and driven into madness, to the dissolution of the self, unable to face reality, plunging into chaos.

The refusal of the corporal dimension, historical, communal and social, can lead to dangerous deviation, not only in the spiritual sphere. It suffices to recall such proposals, be they philosophical, literary or political, that have tried to break the limits considered as negative, to take refuge in a disembodied totality, and the disastrous final results of such proposals.

For example, we can recall the philosophical and existential story of Nietzsche, and his attempt to overlook the boundaries of individuation and identify with the totality of life, with any man, and in the end with God Himself. Exemplary in this respect are the so-called "tickets of madness," that constitute his liberation from ordinary experiences. These "tickets of madness" bear the signature of two characters with which Nietzsche wished to be identified, the two extremes of a whole spectrum of possible personalities, namely Dionysus and the Crucified. However, in this manner "the vessel of individuality," to borrow an expression from Nietzsche himself, ends up wandering adrift into destruction and finally dissolves into chaos. Writing to a friend, Burckardt, a few days before he began sinking into madness, Nietzsche described the condition of identifying with the Absolute in these terms:

> Dear Mr. Professor, in the end, I would much rather be a Professor in Basel than God; but I have not dared thus far to push my private egoism to omit the creation of the world because of him. As you see, one has to make sacrifices, however and wherever one lives. (F. Nietzsche, *Carteggio Nietzsche-Burckhardt*, Boringhieri, Torino 1961, p. 41)

This outcome strikingly resembles the drift of certain thinkers and spiritual currents that equally deny the value of limits and corporality. The refusal of the mediation (of the body) and the rejection of the space-time dimension of the journey of faith manifests itself clearly in the troubled path of Jean Labadie, a French mystic of the seventeenth century:

> To minds like Labadie, the labor of the
> infinite is to subsequently refuse any single
> place. They spend their time 'dissolving'
> themselves from any local identifications.
> This passion of dissolution (of Ab-solute)
> repeats at every step the gesture that
> endlessly says, 'it is not this,' 'it is not this,'
> until they lack the strength. (M. De Certeau,
> *Fabula mistica*, Il Mulino, Bologna 1987, p. 388)

This dedication to the rejection of every
tradition and of any rule considered a betrayal of the
ideal can be compared to the final outcome of the sad
and lonely path of Nietzsche:

> The friend, Overbeck, who rushed from
> Basel to bring home the sick Nietzsche,
> finds him crouched, huddled in a corner of
> the sofa, calm, glazed and seemingly serious,
> speaking in a low voice under the very
> heavy duty hanging over him as a substitute
> for God. (X. Tilliette, *Filosofi di fronte a Cristo*,
> Queriniana, Brescia 1991, p. 286)

Without soil, desired and acknowledged,
without relationships with others and with God, one
is lost. A research carried out in the name of the
rejection of any rules and gradualism, deemed
imperfect and unworthy of the Absolute, the
relationships with others and with God end up
dissolving its members in an introverted vagrancy,
losing even themselves. It is the risk of solitary

49

mystics, the most dangerous in a religious order, a community, a society ... they are reduced to wander without ever finding a land, alone and embittered, finding no place of welcome, no landing point or support.

The final outcome becomes the refusal of all, an autism of a language unable to say anything, the impotence of a desire that no longer leads anywhere. A Flemish mystic of the thirteenth century, Hadewijch, confessed to being possessed by something undefined. He was led to reject any possible mediation, even verbal, because it seemed to diminish the beauty, only to get himself lost in the indefinable. It is the end of one who cannot indicate what he wants because he is too concerned about what he does not want.

As noted in the previous chapter, the experience of God, even the most unexpected and overwhelming, as in the conversion of Ignatius of Loyola or of Paul in Damascus, is led by an integrated desire. Such experience, in addition to a rereading of what happened, requires the maturation of time, usually long and ordinary, marked by successive and gradual steps, such as entering into a community.

Acknowledging the importance of relationships and of time to process and clarify the knowledge of the LORD means being able to keep together two seemingly opposing elements essential to the human existence, namely the value and its historical and communitarian implementation. The decisive criterion that makes this encounter possible does not seem detectable merely on the basis of the human quality and importance of the people who comprise the concrete community in question. This can be seen in Paul's situation where the members of the community, as Paul himself acknowledges, do not seem to excel in human and moral qualities, for among them there were divisions, scandals, immorality and jealousy (cfr. 1Cor 5: 1-2; 11: 20-22). Yet *Paul loves them despite their flaws*, and *it is in them that he has experienced the Lord.* This is not very different indeed from the characteristics of the community instituted by Jesus. The Gospel is not afraid to show the mediocrity, misunderstandings and pettiness of various kinds on the part of the Apostles (cfr. Mk 9: 33-34; 10: 35-37; Acts 1: 6). Nevertheless, it is precisely to them Jesus entrusted the mission of proclaiming salvation to all peoples (cfr. Mt 28: 19-20).

In this contrast, one can highlight the challenge facing every person that sums up the meaning of existence. The most important criterion to realize the value recognized by the desire lies in one's ability to translate the experience in one's own historical and relational context. Thus, the transformation is concretized in works, movements, institutions, in the individual learning to take account of the common person, in the simple actions of ordinary life. (cfr. A. Godin, *Psicologia delle esperienze religiose*, Queriniana, Brescia 1993, p. 88)

This is one of the most valuable lessons of the experience of the Christian life, from which even the most decisive event, namely the Resurrection of Jesus, is not exempt. The resurrection of Jesus is an event hard to accept for the disciple of every age because it is silent, discreet and at the same time profound and intimate. The Resurrection of Jesus gives a profound and inestimable value to everyday life. This could be summed up by the pun of an Italian film of not long ago, *The Last Kiss*. Therein one hears "The real revolution is the norm." The ability to live the ordinary differently is the test for the psychological health of an experience.

The Resurrection of Jesus celebrates a precise way of life. It is the consecration of ordinary life which disputes the search for God in the spectacular. In the *Acts of the Apostles*, Peter recalls how the Risen Jesus has not shown Himself to all, "but to us, the witnesses chosen by God in advance, who ate and drank with Him after He rose from the dead" (10: 41). Eating and drinking are the actions of everyday life, typical of corporeality. They are also the gestures of sharing, of fraternity created by simple but essential activity. It is also significant that the disciples confuse the Risen Jesus with someone else: a gardener (Jn 20: 15), a stranger (Lk 24: 18), a passerby

(Mk 16: 12), a fisherman (Jn 21: 4). He truly has become the common man who is met at every street corner. The same will happen in the final judgment, when Jesus will say to each one,

> [35] For I was hungry and you gave me food, I was thirsty and you gave me drink, a stranger and you welcomed me [36] naked and you clothed me, ill and you cared for me, in prison and you visited me...[40] And the King will say to them in reply, 'Amen, I say to you, whatever you did for one of these least brothers of mine, you did for me.' (Mt 25: 35-36,40)

Language, relations, tradition and community allow spirituality to be translated to an experience accessible to man. The spiritual experience is not the undifferentiated feeling, but the development of the details of the ordinary life, places in which the whole is present. A word, in its limited space of letters, is a sign that speaks of another. If it is deleted it loses its possible indicating element. The spiritual and monastic rules, the teaching of the mystical masters, are part of this essential relationship with the soil, and they provide a valuable aid to recognize the genuineness of such an experience. They reaffirm the importance of gradualism and rules, avoiding the temptation of easy shortcuts or cheap techniques to get hold of the experience of the divine:

> The disciple of a Chinese master went one day to ask him, "How can I achieve enlightenment?" The Master replied, "In the same way that you can make the sun rise." Startled, the disciples responded, "In this case, what use of meditations and ascetic practices?" The Master retorted, "To ensure that, when the sun rises, you are ready." (K. England, *La ricerca psichica tra scienza e fede*, AISP, Modena 1993, p. 128)

This attention given to mediation highlights the possible contributions of psychology, namely to indicate healthy criteria and balance in the awareness of living in a defined and limited space that cannot advance an exclusive claim.

Asceticism and Renunciation, Two Conditions for a Full Life

Why is there tension between the greatness of the ideal and the poverty, sometimes the mediocrity, of its realization? Is it necessary? Can it be avoided? From what has been said thus far, one cannot circumvent the issue. Indeed, it ought to be considered a basic condition, not only of the human experience of God, but also of life in general. It is a place in which the spiritual proposal and psychological reflection meet. It is a fundamental dialectic between desire and limitations.

While the desire, as seen in Chapter One, has the peculiar characteristic of being in continuous expansion, tending to infinity, one observes that the limits of the world proceed in the opposite direction, in a progressive reduction of the possibilities. If at birth one could learn any language, with the passing of time the circle narrows and increasingly bears the scars of past history with its cultural traces, geographical surroundings, acquired habits, mishaps suffered, and choices made. The desire is the blossoming of life that is fresh and blooming while the limits recall the points of no return and the renunciations that characterize one's existence.

The choice of *something* would also imply a *renunciation* of something else. In the decision resides a demand to test the desire, and thus to choose:

> Every act of will is an act of self-limitation. Desiring an action is to desire a limitation. In this sense, every act is an act of self-sacrifice. Choosing one thing is to reject another ... If you become the King of England, you waived the place of caretaker in Brompton. (G.K. Chesterton, *L'Ortodossia*, Morcelliana, Brescia 1980, p. 56)

This is also a profound truth of the spiritual journey: no project, no activity, no person is able to fully satisfy. Every achievement is always partial because it manifests another, a "more."

Acknowledging the limits is very important for the psychological health of a spiritual proposal. For example, in the community in which one lives the religious experience, knowing the existing limits does not mean penalizing the desire for the context of the community remains the only possible way of achieving it. The realization of desire and thus also a fulfilled life, is accomplished through the meeting of the two opposite directions, *desires* and *limitations*. Together they are in dialectical tension in the sense that one refers to the other. On the one hand, one cannot achieve a desire without knowing and coming to terms with the limits. On the other hand, the limits could not be perceived as such if not in the perspective of one's desire to overcome them. Seeing only the desires or only the limits is one-sided, dangerous, and eventually leads to a jaded frustration.

Prohibitions and limitations are indispensable elements of life, confirming the maxim given in Genesis,

> The LORD God gave the man this order: You are free to eat from any of the trees of the garden, except the tree of knowledge of good and evil. From that tree, you shall not eat; when you eat from it you shall die. (Gen 2: 17)

This statement from Genesis is an invitation to recognize one's own reality of being, namely a creature that has received one's existence within precise limits. These limits constitute one's habitat, where one can develop one's potential and realize oneself. The root of the evil in life, which in the Christian tradition is called *original sin* (the original condition that is the basis of every sin done in ordinary life), is found in the refusal of the limits. An immediate consequence of such refusal is the lack of acceptance of oneself. This refusal could be of one's physical and/or intellectual character, of one's own history, culture, origin, hence, longing to be something and/or some else. In this rejection lurks the lack of a realistic self-esteem, which considered psychologically could be analogous to original sin considered in one's own sphere.

This problem may also be present in the apparently opposite behavior. An excessive self-esteem, where one is unable to recognize one's own limits, can in fact become a form of hiding one's frailty, a way to hide the truth that in fact one does not esteem oneself. It is a defense as equally problematic as low self-esteem. Therefore, it is not the supposed presence or absence of finitude that constitute the difficulty, but the assessment in terms of acceptance of oneself. The issue of self-esteem involves, albeit at different levels, every person and reveals the legacy of a deep inner wound.

Finitude is essential for living. This is why it's placed at the beginning of the teaching of biblical wisdom. The limits remind the individual of the fundamental freedom placed at the base of every decision, the suffering that each choice entails, that achieving a good has a price namely the renunciation of other goods. In the end, one has to decide with the awareness that margins of risk are present in every possible choice.

The desire-limit combination in every human reality, although structurally ambiguous, can be of help or lead to destruction. It is helpful when the two movements, opening and closing, are in effective and concrete balance in *the decision*. This balance is an experience of reality, of self-esteem, while the illusion of being all-powerful is an escape that leaves one empty and frustrated. On the one hand, making a decision can be seen as giving up many other possible paths. On the other hand, it can be seen as accomplishing one's decision in a practical and timely manner. Intelligence itself is selective. It does not seek to know everything indiscriminately, but to narrow the field, focusing on what one recognizes as fundamental and worth being pursued, leaving out what is not essential.

Each project, in the moment in which it is executed, has to do with limits. One's choices increase what one has to renounce. To Demmer, *this is the fundamental experience of death* present at every level of one's personal experience manifested through the need for renouncements. A decision implicitly reminds one of the meaning of one's own *death*. Therefore, it requires a horizon of meaning in order to decide (*and renounce*) something important. Hence, one is called to make sense of one's sacrifice if one wishes to realize one's truest and deepest desire. Here one finds the basic foundation for natural asceticism, understood as the need to choose what is essential, what really matters. It also implies the acceptance of death as a fundamental truth of one's existence: Every decision is also a renouncement. The person who decides concretizes by his decision his personal existence and his limitations. One can never realize all the possibilities one has at his disposal. It follows that a situation in which a decision is absolutely clear and free of ambiguity does not exist. (See K. Demmer, *Decision in relation to one's death*, Manoscritto 1974, p. 1)

What looks at first glance as an obvious observation, "I want to do this and therefore I cannot do that," is often the heart of the problem. If the desire is not known, dissected, matured, or the limits are not taken into account or refused as negative, it leaves the person unable to decide. Hence, the fear of a commitment to make a clear choice, especially if the decision is final.

However, when the desire is recognized together with its limits it leads to a real experience because the limits, just as the desire, allow one to live. Think of the precise limits that allow the development of life in an environment: The Earth's axis and the distance from the sun, neither of which can be circumvented because together they create the delicate and precise balance of constants and variables which make life on the earth possible. Beyond these limits there is no life, stability or practicality as we know it. Without these boundaries, there can be no order and no stability. It is no accident that the book of Genesis describes the creation as a series of barriers placed by God that enable various forms of life to develop and spread.

All of this is even more true for a human being. People, as we saw in Chapter One, develop not simply by indulging in what they like but by being educated to overcome obstacles. These obstacles enable the individuals to identify and articulate their capacities. In this battle resides the evaluation of oneself in terms of esteem and deep appreciation as well as opening up the possibility of new initiatives. Being able to recognize one's own limits and respecting them, being aware of situations, places, and experiences in which one's moral and spiritual condition could be at serious risk, helps one grow more and more free, mastering oneself. In the spiritual experience, weaknesses are, paradoxically, precisely those areas in which the person feels stronger and therefore loosens their vigilance. Emblematic is the story of David's sin which begins with a situation of calm and lethargy, both internal and external, from which he will awake too late when he has become an adulterer, a traitor and a murderer (cfr. 2Sam 11: 1-12:14).

Limitations or weaknesses, which exist in everyone, are not the problem as long as they are *explicitly perceived* as such with no need to be denied or covered with various excuses and/or justifications. It is first and foremost a problem of interpretation and evaluation; for this reason, a faculty as seemingly unreal and evanescent as the imagination is decisive (as will be seen in Chapter Three). The preoccupation to present oneself as if without defects and/or to presume to have everything under control is not a good sign of emotional maturity. In fact, such a sign raises serious questions about the authenticity of the spiritual experience. The people which Jesus viewed with great sympathy, the ones who moved Him, were people who were able to recognize their own weaknesses (cfr. Lk 17: 13; 18: 9-14).

Hence, the importance of what is called the "fundamental paradox" of human life: when the dialectic between the desires and limits is recognized, accepted, evaluated in positive terms, and accepted as the only way to realize what is in the heart, it also becomes easier to live. The problems arise when one does not recognize this dynamic and/or tries to eliminate it yielding to the temptation of unilateralism.

Desire and limit are two inseparable aspects of the same component. Together they are information and only in the imagination can they be conceived separately. This is the dangerous side of the imagination, namely the illusion of living without limits and without difficulties. At the base of some tragic gestures, one can find the inability to recognize the limits as an essential character of life.

The Great Enemy of Desire: Fear

The explicit fundamental paradox of our discourse, that often emerges, is the fact that life is a struggle, a path that goes against the grain. To improve one's own situation, whatever it may be, it is in fact necessary to face obstacles and difficulties. Struggling with both entropy and spontaneous disorder characterizes the ordinary situation of human existence. Cleaning up, taking care of oneself, keeping one's room tidy, respecting one's commitments and schedules, properly preparing projects and bringing them to completion, being faithful in relationships and decisions already made are just some examples of this struggle against entropy which tends to grow as much as one abandons oneself to the impulse of the moment. Spirituality must manifest the essential meaning of this tension. The ideal is not to avoid any possible problems and difficulties but to be aware of the importance of the stakes, being willing to get involved in something, or with *Someone*, recognized as the foundation of one's own existence.

In this battle, the obstacle to the desire is not the limits. On the contrary, *the limits manifest the only chance of realizing the desire.* The real enemy is another; it is a sentiment, well known to every person, namely, fear. This shows that the most powerful forces of human life are not logical. For this reason, some choices are made knowing that they will produce harm rather than good.

All this may seem absurd from a purely rational point of view, yet it is often the basis of a dynamic resistance to change: the prospect of improving a situation of hardship and suffering or even healing, can frighten more than encourage, even to the point of giving up. The question Jesus addresses to the paralytic at the pool of Bethesda is not at all obvious: "Do you want to be well?" (Jn 5: 6). Above all, it is an invitation to clarify what is in his heart, to admit that, oddly enough, healing is not the most important thing for him ... and in fact the paralytic does not respond to the question of Jesus but continues to talk about his familiar

63

problems, "Sir, I have no one to put me into the pool when the water is stirred up; while I am on my way, someone else gets down there before me." (Jn 5: 7) These were the problems of the typical day of the paralytic. The resistance to healing is also confirmed in the analytical settings (cfr. S. Freud, *L'io e l'es*, in Id., *Opere*, Boringhieri, Torino 1977, vol. IX, p. 511; Id., *Analisi terminabile e interminabile*, in Id., *Opere*, Boringhieri, Torino 1979, vol. XI, p. 525).

For a change to occur, it is not enough, therefore, to merely "feel bad" or to be exasperated. Above all, one must be convinced, one must have a strong desire to introduce a change in one's life and be willing to pay the price. A disease, an awkward psychological state and the like have an advantage because they provide an answer to some of the person's underlying needs, such as the need for security and stability, or the need to receive affection, support, encouragement and/or attention. Even more rooted masochism has its advantages; otherwise, it would be abandoned. Often in the Gospel, those who are cured do not appear to lead an easier life than before their healing. This is illustrated in the case of the man born blind (cfr. Jn 9), who after being healed is disowned by his parents, threatened by the religious authorities, and expelled from the synagogue. A similar situation occurs with Lazarus resurrected; he is joined to the death sentence decreed for Jesus, "And the chief priests plotted to kill

Lazarus too, because many of the Jews were turning away and believing in Jesus because of him." (Jn 12: 10-11) The crippled man in the third chapter of the *Acts of the Apostles*, having been healed, can no longer receive alms for a living; he has thereby lost his job at the "Beautiful Gate" of the temple which was rightfully his.

"Healing" in the psychological sense, first of all, means to address the fear of losing some definite advantages, to start a new life, healthier and freer, but also a life more uncertain and difficult, of which one does not know the consequences; and for this reason, some changes, even when hypothetically desired are never executed even when the opportunity presents itself.

Fear often presents itself as an all-encompassing, pervasive and "illogical" entity. This can be shown by the strange paradox that characterizes our society. On one side, one sees a situation of unprecedented well-being which allows the individual to easily solve most of the problems related to survival, offering a growing number of people the possibility of nutrition, education and care. On the other side, one sees the excessive pursuit of security evidenced by a dangerous emotional swing from boredom to panic, with radical repercussions to life, especially for the young, that shut down the enthusiasm, the desire, and the will to live:

> Contrary to the objective evidence, those
> who live in a leisure never known before,
> the ones more pampered and more spoiled
> than anyone else in history, are those who
> feel more threatened, insecure, frightened,
> easier to panic and more attracted to
> anything having to do with security and
> safety, than most of the other societies of
> the past and present. (Z. Bauman, *Paura
> liquida*, Laterza, Bari 2008, p. 162)

Fear, when it reigns indiscriminately, has
unpleasant consequences such as sadness, depression,
and a chronic inability to enjoy one's life because one
is obsessed by an evil that does not exist but it could
always manifest itself:

> He who is afraid of being the victim of crime
> runs a double risk of falling into depression
> [...]; fear can also cause a reduction of some
> physical functions affecting the quality of life
> and cause a lower propensity to participate in
> social relations [...]. Reducing this fear can
> probably help improve the mental health of
> many people. (M. Barberi, «Paure (in)
> controllate», in *Mente e cervello* 45 [2008] p. 33)

It is easy to understand how widespread fear
can also be a powerful barrier to the religious
dimension of life. The search for absolute security
obviously does not spare even this sphere of one's
life. Laws and precepts may be fulfilled as a guarantee

of being right with God and with one's conscience without deeply questioning the meaning of one's actions. The tendency to reduce one's relationship with God to a purely legal level is a defense against the underlying fear, not only of one's own frailty and weaknesses, but above all against an unprepared and unpredictable encounter with the mystery of God:

> The chief effect of fear is to build a barricade against the power of love and faith in God. For Jesus, fear and mistrust in God were the greatest enemies of human beings. It suffices to recall the episode of the calming of the storm, when He rebukes the disciples not for lack of virtue, but for being fearful, so that they would realize how much his teaching, from the psychological point of view, aimed at removing man from his own fear. (P. Ionata, «I guai del perfezionismo religioso», in *Città Nuova* 2 [1990] p. 44)

This fearful view of life ends up abolishing the planning dimension, which certainly involves a level of risk, but also of palatability, namely the desire to give oneself to something that is worthy of the gift. This has serious repercussions in other areas of the religious dimension, such as the vocational choice. A document on the situation of vocations in Europe indicated that the presence of excessive security and abundance of goods is causing a serious disorientation among the young, but not only. Reduced to wandering in a thousand different possibilities, but ending up deciding for none for fear of renunciation or failure, with harmful effects on one's self-esteem:

> Many young people are afraid of their future, have anxiety before definitive commitments, and question themselves about their existence... It is a great sadness to meet young people, intelligent and talented, in whom the will to live, the will to believe in something, to work towards great ends, to hope in a world which can become better thanks to their efforts all seems to be extinguished. They are young people who feel themselves *superfluous* to the game or drama of life, almost resigned in the face of it, lost and wounded along the broken paths and reduced to the minimum level of tension in life. Without vocation, without a future, or with a future which, at most, will be a photocopy of the present. (Pontificia Opera per le Vocazioni Ecclesiastiche, *Nuove vocazioni per una nuova Europa*, 8 dicembre 1997, 11c)

The inability to choose, under the illusion that they always have all the options open, makes them more and more slaves to fear, to death. The psychiatrist Yalom noted how the unwillingness to commit to something one feels important strengthens the potential of death in the person by extinguishing more and more the will to live. He writes,

My experience, both professional and personal, has led me to believe that the fear of death is always stronger in those who have the feeling of not having fully lived: the more life was lived poorly, or one's potential wasted, the stronger the fear of death. (I. Yalom, *Guarire d'amore. I casi esemplari di un grande psicoterapeuta*, Rizzoli, Milano 1990, p. 132)

In the *Bible*, fear is the sentiment that most often characterizes the state of mind of a man who is away from God. Fear is the dominant emotion of Adam after sin (Gen 3: 10), Pilate at the time of having to condemn Jesus (Jn 19: 8), and the apostles before the encounter with the Risen Jesus (Jn 20: 19). It was fear that persuaded the unprofitable servant not to use the talent received, burying it (Mt 25: 25), an eloquent image of how this feeling makes one unable to strive for something that is worthy, thus imprisoning the individual in a situation of inner death.

The proliferation of sentiments such as fear indicate that the dimension of trust, of belief and therefore of the religious experience, cannot be replaced with security. On the contrary, the increase of insurance implies an increased sense of instability and insecurity. Faced with the strange balance between safety and fear, science and technology are structurally incapable of providing an adequate response to the most important problems of human existence. This inability reveals an unbridgeable gap, namely the greater the achievements to ensure personal and collective security, the more the symbolic and affective constellations and emotional reactions related to fear increase.

If security does not seem to provide an effective solution, how could it then confront fear? The reflection of the ancients understood that the real enemy to be faced is not outside but inside the human soul because it is spiritual. The real enemy is the fear of fragility, the refusal to accept it: the fear of intimacy that one does not dare share, the fear to trust without knowing whether it is worth it to do so. In the final analysis, the enemy is oneself, as acknowledged in the *Bible* with the teaching on sin: one cannot simply eliminate it, but one ought to come to address it, recognizing and confronting it as such. This is the core of what the tradition, classical and Christian, means by the virtue of courage. It is not the absence of fear, fairly typical of presumption which is an equally dangerous attitude of phobia and anxiety.

Saint Thomas defines courage, *fortitudo mentis*, as the ability to face the full truth, even of danger, without hiding either the difficulties or the possibilities. Only in this way can the truth and/or danger be adequately addressed. The biblical episode of the bronze serpent (cfr. Nm 21:4-9) is an example. (cfr. S. Tommaso d'Aquino, *Summa Theologiae* II-II, q. 123, a.1, Edizioni Paoline, Cinisello Balsamo [Mi] 1975, p. 1580).

Fear and courage are important aspects of the earthly spiritual life. They are implications of the bodily dimension of one's existence. They have the duty to warn one of possible dangers, limitations and fragility, which are the ordinary situations of life. Since risk is a factor in every decision, fear and courage, when employed consciously, are transformed into helpers. They become what the ancients called the virtue of fortitude, the root of courage, which is essential to facing the difficulties of life. The strong person is courageous not because he is ignorant of or denies the danger, but because he can consider his situation realistically and not run away. This ability to stay in the tension between desire and limit, vigilant and aware of frailty and weaknesses, makes courage a virtue typically human, characteristic of a mortal being:

> Fortitude presupposes vulnerability; without vulnerability, there is no possibility of fortitude. An angel cannot be brave, because he is not vulnerable. To be brave actually means to be able to suffer injury. Because man is by nature vulnerable, he can be brave. (J. Pieper, *The Four Cardinal Virtues*, University of Notre Dame Press, Notre Dame, Ind. 1966, p. 117)

The Decision, Antidote to Fear

This analysis invalidates the well-known *cliché* that the brave man knows no fear. This is fairly typical of presumption which constitutes a defect equal and opposite to fear. If courage and fear are not mutually exclusive, their acceptance helps one to evaluate the stakes involved and affords a glimpse at the possibilities of completing an enterprise. The coexistence of fear and courage in human action refers to the need of other equally significant virtues both for the religious experience and the more general context of life, such as patience and temperance, which in turn find their source in hope, the ability to confidently face the difficulties.

Contrary to the suggestions of fear, if one recognizes and accepts the limits one can arrive at a decision, as noted above. Personal maturity is also manifested by one's ability to make decisions, assume responsibilities, and consider the sacrifices and risks involved:

> It has also been shown experimentally that the decision provides three enduring features that are missing in the undecided. The one who decides on the basis of beliefs is more capable of constancy. He is also better able to withstand adversity. Thirdly, the decision enables the person to be more sociable. (A. Manenti, *Vivere gli ideali*, cit., pp. 209-210)

Ignatius recognizes how the enemy of human nature precisely leverages fear to prevent one from choosing the good. Hence, Ignatius is careful to insist that the person be free from this form of slavery in the only way possible, namely by deciding firmly and resolutely:

> As soon as the one leading a spiritual life firmly resists the demon's temptations, acting in a way diametrically opposed to what the demon suggests, it is the demon who becomes weak, loses heart, and abandons the temptation. However, if one begins to fear and lose heart in the face of temptations, there is not a beast in the world so fierce as the enemy of human nature in malicious pursuit of his damned design. (S. Ignazio di Loyola, *Esercizi spirituali* n. 325, cit., pp. 231-232)

This rule finds confirmation in the psychological point of view: the key to effectively fight fear is to avoid being enclosed in one's anxieties. One is to engage life in one's experiences of reality. One is to decide for the values acknowledged as vital for life, even if they cannot be fully accomplished as one would like.

An experiment made in this regard with army paratroopers showed an interesting truth, namely that fear, for those who jump for the first time, reaches its climax in a situation of relative safety. Fear reaches its height in the aircraft cockpit with the word *Ready*! It is the moment when paratroopers are looking forward to the future danger that awaits them. Fear continues to grow until one decides to jump, that is, until one reaches what is called "the point of no return," when one cannot go back, but only fall. Oddly enough, it is precisely from that moment of real danger that fear begins to decrease until it disappears. The authors conclude that when one is confronted for the first time with a difficult task it is natural to feel fear. However, after weighing the possibilities and the risks involved, one decides that it is necessary to "jump" in spite of the fear. In that moment one decides to do what one believes to be the best thing to do. The choice thus enables the individual to cut the knot of fear by stepping into reality. Here one recalls what was said before: one can understand something only by deciding for it, getting involved and taking into account the possible risks. The illusion of having always before oneself, all the possibilities intact or an assurance of absolute security, leaves in the soul, in addition to fear, the feeling of having wasted one's existence.

The strongest antidote to fear remains *the desire*. It is the root of courage and the ability to decide. When the soul is inflamed for an ideal, for a value, for a project of life like falling in love, a conversion, or a vocational decision, while acknowledging one's concerns, fears and difficulties, one is not stopped because of them; rather, they serve as warning signs in one's heart to evoke a force able to face and overcome them with a peace and security never felt before. The desire expressed thus becomes a response to an affectionate and reassuring Presence, even if He is not physically present. When His presence is recognized and accepted, it allows the individual to face situations of objective danger and tension with the confidence of those who feel they are in good hands. "Fear not," Jesus says to Peter, reassuring him in the face of his fears (Lk 5: 10); "Fear not," said the angel to Mary, noting her confusion (Lk 1: 30); "Fear not," Jesus says to the women, *sending them to proclaim the Good News of His Resurrection* (Mt 28: 10).

There is no doubt how much a personal and profound relationship with the Lord constitutes an extremely valuable help in this regard. It points out how one's activity is not the result of chance, but that it fits into a larger project, where the person is never abandoned, especially in the face of difficulties and the unexpected. Here, one recalls the considerations, discussed in Chapter One, namely the importance of *motivation* which is able to give courage and strength and reconfirm the choice identified as good. In this delicate junction, one can recognize the valuable contribution the experience of faith can offer, namely the possibility of finding meaning and energy in the face of what arouses fear. Faith thus presents itself as

Fr. Giovanni Cucci, S.J.

an essential truth of human life, as goes an aphorism of Nietzsche "one who has a why in life can bear almost any how." It is an aphorism that V. Frankl significantly recovers as a discriminating criterion for the autobiographical survival experience described in the book *Man's Search for Meaning.*

Fatigue, suffering and tribulation do not of themselves suggest that it is useless to desire, rather they point to the reality that everything has its price and thus it is important to know "in what to invest one's life." In this situation, the Christian proposal urges the individual to decide for the presence of hope and transcendent love, two decisive elements to experience meaning in life. Both hope and love can help the mental balance of the human being who needs meaning in the same way he needs air to breath.

CHAPTER III: THE CONFIRMATION, IMAGINATION AND SYMBOL

The Power of the Imagination

The conclusion of the previous chapter noted the influence a feeling such as fear can have on the ability to decide. Such an influence can cripple desire and more generally hinder a process based on trust and willingness to participate in something beautiful and attractive. "Do not deceive yourself so you are not disappointed," is the motto of those who seek, above all, to limit the damage they suffer, without ever venturing to participate in life.

Why does fear have such power over our assessments and more particularly over our choices? Because it works in the imagination, focusing on what *could* happen, and this, in terms of confidence and the ability to dare, is often more important than what actually happens. Fear and anxiety are indeed the unspoken message evident in many of the measures we take to protect what we value: armored doors, sophisticated methods of bank security, armed escorts and bodyguards, security cameras, metal detectors and barricades in airports, highways and cities. The imagination suggests to the heart that it is all pointless, that there will always be something or someone who is capable of violating every available protection. These suggestions, in the end, rather than eradicate fear, serve as constant reminder of it. Instead of being a reasonable warning against a concrete danger, they turn fear into unjustified panic that leads to a running away from real life.

Decisions, big or small, are not made on the basis of a procedure of formal and logical measures. To recognize the significant influence that feelings and imagination have on the decision-making process, one need only to think of the criteria with which one reaches ordinary daily decisions, especially those *not* implemented.

Daily activities continuously confirm that evaluative and decision making criteria are linked to processes of our emotions and imagination. Think of this unbelievable story from the news: a cleaner, who had been trapped by mistake in a refrigerator truck, died, frozen to death. In reality, the system was turned off, and the internal temperature never dropped below 18 degrees. This man did not die of cold, but of imagination! (cfr. Ch. Singer, *Del buon uso delle crisi*, Servitium, Sotto il Monte 2006, pp. 58-59) Fantasy can thus be much more real and tangible than physical reality.

Imagination resides at the foundation of our approach to life. It is an essentially interpretative approach, with affective modality, coloring life in terms that are either pleasant or unpleasant, attractive or repulsive, and in which body and spirit are closely united. The imagination is a characteristic proper to the spirit because it has the inherent power to make present what is physically absent, thereby placing itself on a higher level of perception than the here and now and what is empirically determined. It is thanks to the quality of the imagination that one projects the near future, fantasizing about what one will do in an hour or in a day. It is always the imagination that makes one's desire virtually infinite, unbounded, always placing a beyond and more to its possible realizations, as seen in previous chapters.

The example of the news mentioned above also highlights the practical and concrete character of

Fr. Giovanni Cucci, S.J.

the imagination because it engages feelings and images, which in turn influence the mind and the will, the locations par excellence of one's assessment and decision making. The imagination presents to the mind and will a unified direction, which is the basis of every thought, plan and action. For this reason, the imagination can be considered a place of encounter among the various faculties of the person, in which body and spirit interact, referring to each other:

> The search for a road or for a book on the shelf or for a friend on the corner are very simple operations; yet they need the function of the imaginative, its synthesis and its winding capacity. (V. MELCHIORRE, *L'immaginazione simbolica*, Il Mulino, Bologna 1972, p. 32)

One can thus appreciate the enormous influence a faculty such as the imagination has on human life, and the importance of its education and discipline. One's imagination can in fact lead the individual to the rejection of reality, making one submissive to one's fantasies, reassuring perhaps but false. Such a one ends up imprisoned by one's own ghosts. When this powerful faculty is educated, consciously considering what represents the horizon of the world, it brings undoubted benefits, even on the somatic component of the person, allowing a person to deal more effectively with various situations and difficulties. A simple but significant experiment recently confirmed how the imagination, deliberately evoked and exercised with regular practice, affects not only the representation of the environment but one's physical being. A group of individuals, selected at random, was to perform a series of movements with the little finger for a month, 5 times per week. Another group was simply to imagine the same exercise for the same length of time. After the experiment, there was noted a physical strengthening of the muscle in both groups, 30% in those who physically carried out the exercise, and 22% in those who had only imagined doing so (cfr. CH. FRITH, *Inventare la mente. Come il cervello crea la nostra vita mentale*, Cortina, Milano 2009, p. 134).

The imagination manifests itself as a very real and powerful faculty, able to involve the whole person, spirit and body, taking one to extreme and radical choices until death. Hence, rationally, the *cliché* that logic is the most precise and effective way to grasp reality must be denied:

> Man's historicity, his planning capabilities, including judgment, memory and prediction, could not exist without the unifying ability of his own imagination. (V. Melchiorre, «Immaginazione», in *Enciclopedia filosofica*, Bompiani, Milano 2006, vol. VI, p. 5539)

The power of imagination highlights the limits of a rationalistic conception of life which tends to identify knowledge with purely abstract processes. Although it has the charm of a simple and coherent proposal, this vision shows itself unable to account for the complexity of human reasoning which is present in a relevant way in both the emotions and the unconscious. The bodily characteristic of perception, expressed by the dialectical perspective-horizon (cfr. Chapter Two), can also be recognized in one's assessment: a human being thinks and judges on the basis of imaginative-affective models (partly unconscious) with which one depicts reality and on the basis of these iconic elements later makes decisions: In general, the world that constitutes our conscious minds is a sequence of representations that result from a series of processes, and the world in our unconscious mind is the same series of processes. It contains some representations of which we are unaware. In other words, all mental processes are unconscious. At best, we are aware of some of the results. (See P. Johnson-Laird, *How We Reason*, Oxford University Press, New York 2006, p. 53)

Therefore, the "rational" person, in the sense of purely formal logic, does not exist. The human mode of thinking is very different from the logical-track procedure, such as the one programmed on a computer. In fact, logic alone almost never has a decisive role in the more important and delicate general issues of everyday life unless after the fact in "things already done." The decisive factor is rather the contribution of imagination and affections:

> The fictitious creations of our mind affect our psychic functions in the same normative power as the people 'in the flesh and blood' that surround us. Without these imaginary realities, human life becomes a dull animal existence. (A. Rizzuto, *La nascita del Dio vivente*, cit., pp. 82-83)

This is why some forms of virtual addiction, such as pornography on the internet, are so utterly devastating. While they stimulate the imagination, being virtually infinite, one ends up losing all limits. This process leads to the annihilation of the person who enters into this dynamic as one feels less and less the call of physical reality: i.e. the feeling of hunger, thirst and/or need for sleep. Instead, one finds oneself unable to perform commitments of relational or affective character, to the point of dying of starvation caused by one's inability to "disconnect" from the charm of the virtual world (Some actual cases are presented in G. Cucci, *Paradiso virtuale o infer.net? Rischi e opportunità della rivoluzione digitale*, Roma-Milano, Ancora-La Civiltà Cattolica, 2015, p. 10-11).

Imagination and Religious Experience

In light of these considerations it is not difficult to understand how critical this power proves to be in one's relationship with God. It is one of the most effective representations of the Absolute, essentially formulated in terms of attraction or repulsion, of affective response to Him. Some problems with one's relationship with God are expressions of profound difficulties that lie ultimately in one's ideal world.

> Pathological unconscious fantasies deeply affect the subject's ability to love, to have intimacy with others, to have an appropriate self-esteem, to work, and even to conceive a benevolent God. (A. Rizzuto, *«Capacità di credere. Considerazioni psicologiche sulla funzione del credere nello sviluppo personale e religioso»*, [*manoscritto*] 2007, p. 5)

Hence, the importance of working on self-knowledge which is essential for the spiritual life. When one's affections and imagination are educated, consciously evaluated, and confronted with one's personal history, highlighting one's reference values, they can reveal the profound truth of the person and what one really seeks in one's ordinary choices, as noted in Chapter One.

From what has been said thus far one can go a step further: a change becomes truly profound and effective when it involves the imagination because it is then that the whole of one's inner world begins to change. Perhaps, up to now, not enough attention has been given to the role imagination occupies (and has occupied) in the spiritual experience for fear of reducing the experience of God, and so God Himself, to a sort of untouchable fantasy, a psychoanalytic illusion.

The spiritual masters were well aware of the importance of the imagination. As mentioned above, Saint Ignatius explains how the enemy of human nature seeks to paralyze the freedom and the desire of those who would do the will of God through the imagination and fear, exaggerating the risks and the difficulties so that the individuals do not choose the good (cfr. S. Ignazio di Loyola, *Esercizi spirituali* n. 315, cit., p. 223). Hence, one understands the care Saint Ignatius prescribes to regulate the imagination, consciously inspiring it, starting from the reading of a text, stimulating the intellect and the understanding, and then nudging the will toward a corresponding reformation of life. This link between reading and imagination strengthens one's desire, counteracts the fear, and gives rise to profound healing. As noted by Durand, visualizing a situation, especially one charged with anguish or danger, is already an effective way to control it since it reveals one's ability to integrate it with other components. When imagination is placed in dialogue with the different faculties of the individual, it can stimulate thought and action rather than blocking them. This is why St. Ignatius places in the *Spiritual Exercises* appropriate explanatory notes, "Additions," which have the task of explaining and educating the imagination, deepening the internalization of the Scripture when it is read or heard. For Ignatius, becoming aware of the feelings that the reading of the sacred text evokes helps the individual understand what the Lord wants, hence, identifying a path of life.

The re-reading of one's life in the light of God's Word allows one to recognize new meanings in what has been lived in the past, breaking any vicious cycles that might otherwise block the way. This ability to place oneself at a distance from the immediate lived experience helps one to recapture the action and to read it as one does a text, showing one the possibilities and opportunities being missed or disregarded but nevertheless still present in it. Every story, when told anew, can show unexpected new possibilities and teachings, opening up the future and thus becoming a reason for hope:

> Being able to recount a feeling, being able to represent it, means that it ceases to be hate, anger, or even love, in pure and immeasurable shape, but becomes a representation of that. (G. Martini, *Ermeneutica e narrazione*, Boringhieri, Torino 1998, p. 320)

This spiritual conception of the reading denies a cultural climate that, in the name of an ambiguous *laissez-faire*, believes that the imagination knows no rules or discipline, leaving the person lost, at the mercy of superficiality and the emotion of the moment. On the contrary, St. Ignatius, reflecting on his conversion story, understood very well the role that this power had in identifying the steps within the new path that was opening before him. Through the imagination, he could relive the scene narrated by the text and actualize it in his own life. Visual representations evoked by the word of God can educate the mind and speak to the heart, actualizing in prayer the invitation extended to us by Saint Paul to have "the same attitude that is also yours in Christ Jesus." (Phil 2: 5)

For Saint Ignatius, God's word actually changes the person when it stimulates the imagination, speaking to the life of the reader. This was his fundamental experience of God, awakened, as we have seen, from a reading that was able to touch the heart, raising the possibility of projects and major decisions for the Lord. This is why Ignatius suggests in the *Spiritual Exercises* that when one is presented with episodes from the life of Jesus, one ought to always represent the scene visually, what we call *the composition of place*:

> Seeing in the imagination the material place
> where is found what I want to

contemplate: for example, the temple or a mountain where Jesus Christ or Our Lady is found. In the contemplation or meditation of a non-sensible reality, as in the case of sins, the composition will be to see with the imagination and consider my soul imprisoned in this mortal body, and the whole man as an exile in this valley between dumb animals: the whole man, means soul and body. (S. Ignazio di Loyola, *Esercizi spirituali* n. 47, cit. p. 73)

Day dreaming and imagination, when "evangelized," can in turn become a powerful help because the Holy Scripture comes to heal the deepest dimension, the unconscious:

That man can also make use of the imagination in his discovery of God, it is sometimes necessary to resort to strong and vigorous images, and to spend some time in the gazing at these images to set in motion the imagination as well as the place of projection in the unconscious. (P. H. Kolvenbach, Folli per Cristo. La sapienza di Maestro Ignazio, Borla, Roma 1999, p. 67)

Behind these cautions found in the *Additions* in the *Spiritual Exercises*, one notes an educational itinerary, which stems from a precise knowledge of the reading, both relational and interactive, asking the individual to enter into and participate in the scene presented by the text, more than generalizing from concepts. In the Ignatian reading of the sacred text, what truly matters is not acquiring new information so much as paying attention to the emotional aspect of the story. This level of encounter can be achieved when one "enters" into the scene, engaging the senses. It is an "incarnated" reading because the spirit, without the flesh and blood, is not nothing as Saint John would say. (cf. 1Jn 5: 6)

A tale of life, as already noted by Ricoeur, speaks to the life of the reader. It helps one understand one's existential story, manifesting new possible routes. This conception of the book and its reader can be reached through what the French philosopher called *narrative identity*: one understands only when telling it to another, recognizing what one was seeking to understand from the lived experience. It is the overall design, the overall context of the narrative that indicates its possible truth, that which may manifest itself as the thread running through the narrative (Ricoeur) or the end point of the train of thought (Ignatius). All of this has a highly regenerative value from a human and spiritual point of view. Critically examining one's motives and exploring the quality of the imaginative inner world become easier when revisited. Thus, in addition to being reconciled with the wounds of the past, the person is opened to the dimension of mystery, to a larger world that is experienced as benevolent. These are the fruits of the goodness and generosity of the Lord, who invites us to trust.

It is a reading done on several levels, yet at the same time unified. It is a reading that allows one to "enter" more effectively into the contemplation of the mystery by involving the three faculties of the spirit: memory, which brings to mind the story told; the intellect, which identifies the most important elements capable of speaking to the life of the reader; and the will, which raises and acknowledges the corresponding affections (cfr. S. Ignazio di Loyola, *Esercizi spirituali* nn. 50-51, cit., pp. 76-78). The point of arrival, the "fruit" to be harvested from the text and followed, is the ability to recognize and implement major changes in one's life by the transformation of one's image of God. The Ignatian imagination is not satisfied with its own images which are more or less fictitious, but seeks to be placed on the *Way* as in the passage of the magi (cfr. Mt 2). It triggers a dynamism which, involving all of one's faculties, allows the individual to reform one's life. The contemplations of the *Spiritual Exercises* do not have a static scene, but an itinerary: "the way from Nazareth to Bethlehem" (n. 112, p. 115), "the road from Bethany to Jerusalem" (n. 192, p. 155), "the way from Mount Zion to the valley of Jehoshaphat" (n. 202, p. 160), and "from the house of Pilate up to the crucifixion" (n. 208, pp. 161-162). It is an itinerary that questions the life of the prayerful person, suggesting appropriate changes. If the reader can recognize and rework, reprocess all of this, then he can become more and more the author of his life, actively collaborating with what is moving inside of him. (cfr. A. Spadaro, *Abitare nella possibilità*, Jaca Book, Milano 2008, pp. 155-159)

Many times the affective and imaginative reading of a text has changed the life of the reader. Consider the experience of Saint Augustine who picked up the *Bible* at the height of his crisis and came across the text of Paul's Letter to the Romans. Recall the experience of the already mentioned Edith Stein who, after a night spent reading the autobiography of Teresa of Avila, decided to ask for Baptism. These are cases and situations very distant from one another in time but united by this type of interactive reading in which one life speaks to another life, where like recognizes like. "I found it!" said Stein at the end of her reading, an understanding that simultaneously became a conversion, recognizing a presence both beyond and at the same time intimate. It was the truth observed by Gregory the Great, "Sacred Scripture grows with those who read it." (*Omelie su Ezechiele* I, VII, 8, in *Opere di Gregorio Magno*, Città Nuova, Roma 1992, p. 215)

The act of reading the word leads to a situation already experienced which the reader clarifies and explicates before the text. For some, as in the examples above, it was also an unexpected encounter with the mystery of God. This experience of the reading leads to the same conclusion as that is reached in the previous chapters: the presence of God is recognized not by fleeing from one's life and history. God is to be recognized right inside one's life, as part of a narrative that has the power to speak in a particularly effective and incisive way to the events of the reader and the narrator. God is found in ordinary daily activity by reflecting on its silent and hidden dynamics, exercising the gifts offered by the corporeal reality.

For Ignatius, this narrative meeting between reading, feelings and a life project is condensed in a symbolic word: *Jerusalem*. His conception of *Jerusalem* meant more than a city. It signified for Ignatius a new state of life, the goal of a journey, the realization of a desire to do something good for the LORD thus making even his own existence so beautiful.

The Symbol, Key to the Mystery of God

Both the imagination and the affections are concretized in symbols, another important element in the spiritual life. The symbol, as in the above-mentioned example of *Jerusalem* is able to concentrate in a word, in an image, the dynamic of a lifetime. Seen in this perspective, the characteristic of the symbol is first of all *affective*. Think of some basic symbols such as the words "father" and "mother." These are capable of arousing overwhelming memories of the past: suffering, joy, nostalgia, along with inner movements that sometimes absorb the thoughts and activities of the day entirely. Affection is an essential component of the symbol that distinguishes it from the concept, from the idea. Qualifying the value on a personal level, affection makes the symbol more relative but also more concrete. In fact, we decide on the basis of symbols, especially on the basis of the attraction or the repulsion they evoke in us. This does not mean that the reflexive and cognitive components do not enter into play as well, but the certainty of the resolution resides in the affective.

Having as an essential characteristic the elicitation of an emotional response in the individual, the symbol cannot therefore be explained by the laws of logic. The laws of the imagination and feeling suffice. This is why, unlike the concept or idea, the symbol can hold together (this is the literal meaning of *sim-bolo*) contrasting elements because in the field of affection the principle of non-contradiction does not enter into play. The same reality can arouse both love and hate; hence, it is lived with a sense of conflict, of inner laceration that makes choosing difficult:

Fr. Giovanni Cucci, S.J.

> the symbol therefore has the power to recognize and express what the logical discourse detests: the demands of tensions, incompatibilities, conflicts, struggles, and internal destruction until it satisfies a need that these refinements are not able to meet. (B. Lonergan, *Il metodo in teologia*, cit., p. 86)

From this point of view, one can say that there is nothing "neutral" in our lives, even the seemingly most aseptic item (a railroad car, an ashtray, a bench, a calculator) can communicate a great deal from a symbolic-affective point of view.

The symbol, being closely tied to the imagination, also has a strong influence on one's life because it has to do with feelings which lead one to action, to making a choice. The English writer C.S. Lewis shows effectively the failure of pure rationalism with regard to concrete choices:

> In battle it is not syllogisms that will keep the reluctant nerves and muscles to their post in the third hour of the bombardment. The crudest sentimentalism (such as Gaius and Titius would wince at) about a flag or a country or a regiment will be of more use ... The Chest-Magnanimity-Sentiment — these are the indispensable liaison officers between cerebral man and visceral man. It may even be said that it is

94

by this middle element that man is man:
for by his intellect he is mere spirit and by
his appetite mere animal. (C.S. Lewis,
L'abolizione dell'uomo, Jaca Book, Milano
1979, pp. 29-30)

However, the emotional life is not necessarily
in conflict with rationality. In fact, between the two
exists a fundamental relationship of harmony which is
essential for life in its various dimensions; indeed, it is
required. If conflict between them seems at times
inevitable, it is because the value and the sentiment
look at different objects, as in situations when one is
called to suffer for living harmoniously one's own
choice or for the beloved.

The symbol can be considered one of the
most important expressions to speak of the Absolute
in the simple brevity of a sentence. In the immediacy
of an image one can fit the extremely large and the
extremely small. This is a typical style of the biblical
God and it is captured well by the anonymous author
of the sepulchral eulogy of St. Ignatius of Loyola: *non
coerceri maximo, contineri tamen a minimo, divinum est* (not
to be restrained by the greatest, but to be bound by
the least is divine).

The symbol, as a language that refers to
something else, shows the importance of *signs* in the
experience of God. Those who have known Jesus in
the Gospels have "seen the man and believed God"

(St. Augustine); they read the sign and made a synthesis, from the sign to its interpretation and to the trust in the one who performed it; "the interior experience of God or the recognition of the Spirit is always indirect, mediated by signs interpreted ultimately by the faith" (Godin). These are the signs present in life which are to be interpreted, for they refer to a greater reality, never completely circumscribed, a reference that we have not created because the manner in which they occur do not depend on us. Nevertheless, they can be recognized and accepted.

The symbol has the power of making the invisible visible, even on a narrative level, as in the account of a parable. In a parable, the mystery of the Kingdom of God is present starting from ordinary experience and spontaneously maintaining a paradoxical distance from the usual criteria of evaluations and behaviors. A parable teases the intellect by starting with something seemingly obvious but then, with the progress of the discourse, manifesting bizarre and incongruous development, even though the continuity of the narrative keeps it from becoming absurd. A parable speaks of a normal situation in nature, well known to all, and applies it to human life leading to paradoxical consequences. For example, the story of the seed and the seasons, with its basic and universal symbols, helps one understand the mysteries of the Kingdom of God: the seed bears fruit when it dies, so it is with the life of Jesus and of the disciple, one can only receive the life given to others (cfr. Jn 12: 24-25).

The *Bible* presents the reality of God in His inaccessible mystery in symbolic form. Consider, among many examples, the opening of Psalm 104, where God is described by many symbols:

> [2] ... You spread out the heavens like a tent; [3] setting the beams of your chambers upon the waters. You make the clouds your chariot; traveling on the wings of the wind. [4] You make the winds your messengers; flaming fire, your ministers. [5] You fixed the earth on its foundation, so it can never be shaken. [6] The deeps covered it like a garment; above the mountains stood the waters. [7] At your rebuke they took flight; at the sound of your thunder they fled. (Ps. 104: 2-7)

Scripture often invites the reader to reflect on the signs present in nature so that the reader can reason by analogy and recognize the Author (cf. Wisdom 13: 1-5; Rom 1: 19-23). St. Thomas, referring to biblical teaching, sees in the analogy a chance to say something true about God, starting from the experience of created reality. This mode of thinking makes it possible to recognize the similarities between different realities without denying their differences. (cfr. *Summa Theologiae* I, q. 13, aa. 1-2.5, cit., pp. 60-62.64-65)

Symbolic language becomes the most appropriate mode to express the experience of God in words. Similarly, a parable is able to pass from one situation to another, starting from the element with which it is connected together and then placed on another unexpected level.

Images and narratives are powerful educational tools because they remain deeply engraved in the listener, making it easy to retain the event in one's memory. Parables report episodes that attract attention. They speak to the listener's life and show that despite the diversity of the situations narrated there is something that unites them, namely the style of God at work. In the biblical perspective man becomes the highest symbol of the sacred in his life: "As a symbol the man ... is both the appearance and the hiding place of an absolute that calls him and already constitutes him." (V. Melchiorre, *Metacritica dell'eros*, Vita e Pensiero, Milano 1977, pp. 70-71)

The Crisis of the Religious Sense: do the Heavens Still Declare the Glory of God?

It has been repeatedly pointed out that the element of corporeality proves decisive in an integral and balanced spirituality in accordance with the principle of the Incarnation. This bodily feature is certainly found in the symbols present in the theological language: think of the role that sexuality and love have always played in expressing the relationship between God and humanity at the biblical-spiritual level, particularly in the mystical experience.

The Song of Songs presents the search for God in essentially body-affective terms related to sexuality. The search is expressed in the symbol of the beloved who is searching with painful nostalgia for the Beloved who was once known but now is lost. The erotic narrative expresses the essential characteristic of the symbol in its fullest form, in its intentional duality: to say and not say, to allude to another, requiring a priori taste for interpretation, fascination with the enigma and respect for the mysterious dimension present in this existence.

However, when one attempts to reduce a symbol to the verifiable, to its technical codification, avoiding the risk of interpretation, one loses it, degrading it to pure information. If it is seen as the claim to absolute security concealing within itself a deadly drift, it makes it impossible to fully live and chose; rather the more the people look for certainty the fear increases and irrational behavior increase. The philosopher Descartes, the so called the father of modernity, places absolute clarity as the criteria of truth. In this way, he excluded any possible doubt and uncertainty. This criterion, however, applied to religious experience, leads to the impossibility of access to its own proper language and horizon; it remains a mute language because the key is lost.

Think of the cultural consequences of the present misunderstanding of marriage symbols: the affective imagination of the relationship is less and less present in them and this has impacted the religious experience and the representation of the sacred. In this respect Singer observes,

> Sexuality is always a manifestation of the sacred. Through this door man and woman have access to the resonance of creation. When a society wants to separate man from his transcendence, it does not need to attack the great buildings of the churches or religions, it suffices to degrade the relationship between man and woman. (Ch. Singer, *Del buon uso delle crisi*, cit., p. 47.)

Without the evocative power of the symbol, the religious language and the richness of the poem of eros itself are undermined. Human sexuality is essentially a cultural-interpretative fact. The highest forms of expression of human sexuality reside in allusions, images, symbols and signs. If these are completely revealed they lose their evocative power and are flattened out to the purely horizontal level of empty and mundane skills. Corporeality, relationship, love and religious sense walk together hand in hand. The book of *Genesis* recognized that the most appropriate image of God present in creation is detectable in the male-female relationship (cfr. Genesis 1: 27); when this loses its essential symbolic reference, it leads to the loss of the ties of which the image was the guardian, namely the God-man relationship and the man-woman relationship, sharing the experience of love. Pascal insightfully noted the reversibility of John's saying, "God is love", commenting that if there is love there is God. Similarly, the crisis of one carries within it the crisis of the other. Religion and eroticism become emptied of content and the possibility of comprehension: The language of the *Song of Songs* and that of his interpreters do not seem to awaken the imagination of our contemporaries as it awakened the minds and the hearts of the men and women mystics of times past. Hence, it is legitimate to ask whether a culture in which explicit sex has invaded almost every aspect of communication, entertainment and advertising can still make effective use of the erotic imagination in religious literature. (See K. EGAN, "Eros, Friendship and love. The Future of Bridal Mysticism," in *Studies in Spirituality* 16 [2006] 138)

The loss of this symbolic richness highlights a cultural crisis, not only religious, which in turn manifests itself in the hermeneutics and the human sciences, reducing communication, as Heidegger would say, to its technical and informative modality.

This misunderstanding has its roots in ancient times, and retracing the historical events related to it is not the focus of this book. Nevertheless, a Christian writer of the third century, Origen, tried to spiritualize the language of eros, reducing it allegorically to the soul's journey to the divine life. This attempt has an impressive line of continuity with some of today's reading approaches to human sexuality ranging from "virtual" interpretation to "animalistic" eros. The phenomenon of the internet addiction already mentioned represents only the latest link in a long chain of diminishing the bodily and symbolic dimension of love. However, it is significant to note that the tendency to deny the value of human corporeality in the religious sphere proper to some Platonic spiritualistic currents, led to the crisis of the relationship with God and resulted in the same excesses of materialism. If the characteristic elements of human love have nothing to do with God, what sense would there be in expressing the mystery with symbols of love?

> The human eros could not speak of divine love if it could not already bring about its [humanity's] own intimacy [...]. To say that Israel is "wife and sister," refusing or concealing the original meaning of "wife" and "sister" is to advance insignificance [to advance nothingness] or *flatus vocis*. Therefore, for the tradition of the bridal language to have some religious sense, it

can only be collected from the original
meaning of marriage and, more generally,
only starting from the essential ways of the
eros. (V. Melchiorre, *Metacritica dell'eros*, cit.,
pp. 37-38)

The previous considerations return here,
namely the link between desire and limits. This
includes the longing for the Absolute and the need
for the experience to be rooted in one's own land, in
one's own story, so that the experience of God can be
effective. The religious symbolism of eros concretely
expressed by the male-female relationship, despite
coming from a different level of meaning, speaks of
the same idea, namely the critical need to remain in
dialectical tension, whether it be between desire-limit,
infinity-historicity or equality-difference. This duality
can help keep the tension between finite-infinite,
horizontal-vertical, man-God, without falling into the
temptation of eliminating one of the two elements
involved. And this is precisely the symbolic eros:
Love lives in this dialectical polarity eros-death,
creativity-norm, rebellions-roots.

The wealth of the balance present in the
tension between opposites is not only true of the
eros. It is repeatedly seen that it constitutes a valuable
psychological truth of existence. Reclaiming and re-
reading the symbolic richness in which the spiritual
tradition, male and female, spoke of God, of love, of
the depths of man and woman is an urgent task so

that both symbolic and analogical thought can regain a credible channel of expression, able to manifest and to respect the essential dualities of attraction and tension, refer and possess, home and journey which are proper of eros.

In this manner, an experience of God can find its most authentic documented expression and spontaneously become a phenomenon of criticism and protest: It denounces a superficial and reductive conception of human existence that, in the name of the useful and profitable, has lost the ability to marvel at one's being-in-the-world. It is no coincidence that wonder was, for the ancients, the fundamental attitude towards the religious experience and wisdom. This is exactly what gives flavor and taste to life, pointing to a sense of direction and meaning.

Conclusion: In what God/god does one believe?

The underlying unity manifested by the complexity of the issues raised in the experience of God (desire, affections, relationships, reading, history, imagination, landmark, symbol, eros), can be grasped indirectly when considering how some life situations, while not explicitly touching religious themes, often present their significance when retraced to some of these privileged places. This essentially was Ignatius' experience of and his entry into a world unknown to him up to that point in his life. He gained access through an ordinary life experience, in this case reading. Hence, it can be concluded that some basic elements of the relationship with God and of a possible representation of it manifest the essential characteristics of every human, although not explicitly acknowledged. It is possible to say that every life story has to do, like it or not, with a representation of God:

> Desires, defenses and fears all contribute to shaping the material of which is made the representation of God. As long as man retains his capacity to symbolize, imagine and create superhuman beings, God will always be in the subconscious at least. (A. Rizzuto, *La nascita del Dio vivente*, cit., p. 91)

These conclusions solicit a question of enormous practical significance: if the symbolic experience of eros, which is an expression of the loving relationship, can be recognized as the most suitable representative place to discover the presence of God in one's life, how many can say they have recognized a link (*sim-bolo*) between the two experiences? Unfortunately for many people, even believers and participants, this is not the case. For many individuals, the representation of God is associated with other affective modalities, such as fear, shame and guilt and/or magical thoughts about the interpretation of the events such as the crime-punishment combination on occasions of misfortune and natural disasters.

Too often the religious experience has been reduced to a purely informative modality, simply to know whether God exists. The Gospel, denouncing the superficiality of such an approach, invites us deeper into the complexity, far beyond possible partisan factions or declarations of principles which do not seem to be of any interest. It is not enough to say, "Lord, Lord" to be automatically admitted into the category of believers (Mt 7: 21-23), nor is a refusal in and of itself a proof of disbelief (Mt 21: 30). The question of God has to do with a much more complex dimension than that of speculation and reasoning, of affirmation or denial:

> A dear friend, an unbeliever, told me that the existence of a Creator is part of the evidence of things, just as it is clear that this book was written by someone. But, he added, the problem for me is that I am not in love with Him; I do not feel Him deeply connected to my life. It is exactly here [that we have] the knot of faith. In that sense, one could say that love comes "before" faith. (V. Paglia, *La via dell'amore*, San Paolo, Cinisello Balsamo [Mi] 2007, pp. 10-11)

The disciple himself, as presented in the Gospel, is not immune to the risks entailed by having the legalistic mindset rather than the affective one. Think of the episode in which Jesus is questioned by his own apostles about the possible guilt of the man born blind, as if this were the only possible reading of the man's blindness. Jesus clearly excludes any link between sin and the calamity of the man, declaring, "Neither he nor his parents sinned; it is so that the works of God might be made visible through him." (Jn 9: 3) Jesus heals him, confirming that it is not a question of the will of God. God always wants goodness to triumph over evil. The gospel unequivocally rejects any persistent and hard to die association, between physical suffering and divine punishment, no matter how powerfully and obstinately it is presented. The death of Jesus, the innocent victim, on the Cross remains the most radical challenge to the axiom crime-punishment.

Yet such a reading resurfaces regularly during painful events: the guilt and the interpretation of what happened in a magic-punitive way remains deeply rooted in the human psyche, contradicting centuries of preaching and religious education.

This "ancestral" tendency to reduce the relationship with God to a fatalistic level of cause and effect can also constitute a form of defense against the fear of an unsettling and unpredictable encounter with the mystery of God. He is greater than one's criteria, greater than one's own fear or wisdom, and therefore the encounter is all the more unsettling.

Hence, the importance of a conversion even from one's psychological representation of God. A conversion which will connect one's representation of God to attributes and feelings other than fear and superficial judgment, aiming at a conversion of the ideal and an imaginary world. As observed by Godin, if man can be said naturally religious, he is never naturally Christian. Anyone who reflects honestly can find within himself both the believer and the unbeliever. Both are called to find a way of listening, of dialogue and mutual education, even when torn between the possible readings of the signs and the reluctance to follow them because one is afraid to pay the price. Significant in this regard is the admission of Cardinal Martini, at the opening of the famous series of lectures entitled *The Chair of the Unbelievers*:

> The non-believer in me disturbs the believer in me and vice versa [...]. I believe that, in our times, the presence of non-believers who sincerely declare themselves as such, and the presence of the believers who have the patience to want to return to themselves, can be very helpful to one another because it stimulates each of us to better follow his path towards authenticity. Performing this exercise, with vulnerability

and radical honesty, may also be useful to a
society that is afraid to look within and that
is likely to live in insecurity and discontent.
(C.M. Martini, *Cattedra dei non credenti*,
Rusconi, Milano 1992, pp. 5-6)

In this dialogue, within and outside of oneself, the word and the reflection of the non-believer prove to be equally valuable and instructive, for it reveals a question that disturbs one's peace and cannot be cheaply silenced, but must be considered with intelligence and sincerity. A famous anthropologist admitted to not believing in God, but he also admitted to being continually troubled: if he were to single out a symbol with which to represent Him, he would choose a shell, a fossil that even if buried under the earth for millions of years can still be placed on one's ear and bring the echo of the distant sea. Similarly, he added, God is a voice of this type, which speaks of mystery greater than us that nothing can erase because it is imprinted in the depths of our being and that sometimes resurfaces when He is least expected, if only by the suspicion that there might be ...

It is an important confession because it reflects the situation of the disciple described in the Gospel: the path of psychological, intellectual and spiritual maturity in the life of faith does not disregard questions and doubts, but invites one to enter into their complexity, eschewing easy ideological labels. In the Gospel, faith and unbelief are not mutually exclusive. Believing is not synonymous with absolute certainty. Faith does not exempt the believer from doubt. The disciples are often reproached by Jesus because they do not understand or for their lack of faith, a refrain that characterizes the entire Gospel of Mark (4: 40; 5: 36; 6: 52; 7: 18; 8: 21; 9: 23 ...) and more benignly, as in the gospel of Matthew, because of their *oligopistìa*, little faith.

The elements which emerged from these pages, despite the variety of situations, stories and events, seem to indicate the same direction, namely the importance of reading the signs of one's life, seeing and entering the profound truth of oneself. This is a struggle from which no one can be excused if one wishes to recognize the places in which the Mystery manifests Himself, as St. Augustine would say, "closer to me than I am to myself" (*Le confessioni*, III, 6, 11, Città Nuova, Roma, 1982, p. 67).

BIBLIOGRAPHY

Agostino, s., *Le confessioni*, Città Nuova, Roma, 1982.

Barberi, M., «Paure (in)controllate», in *Mente e cervello* 45 (2008) 29-35.

Bauman, Z., *Paura liquida*, Laterza, Bari 2008.

Cencini, A., *Nell'amore. Libertà e maturità affettiva nel celibato consacrato*, EDB, Bologna 1995.

Certeau (De), M., *Fabula mistica. La spiritualità religiosa tra il XVI e il XVII secolo*, Il Mulino, Bologna 1987.

Chesterton, G.K., *L'Ortodossia*, Morcelliana, Brescia 1980.

Cucci, G., *La forza della debolezza. Aspetti psicologici della vita spirituale*, AdP, Roma 2007.

_____, *Esperienza religiosa e psicologia*, Elledici-La Civiltà Cattolica, Leumann-Roma 2009.

Demmer, K., *Decision in relation to one's death*, Manoscritto 1974.

Egan, K., «Eros, Friendship and love. The Future of Bridal Mysticism», in *Studies in Spirituality* 16 (2006) 131-150.

England, K., *La ricerca psichica tra scienza e fede*, AISP, Modena 1993.

Freud, S., *L'io e l'es*, in Id., *Opere*, Boringhieri, Torino 1977, vol. IX, 469-520.

_____, *Analisi terminabile e interminabile*, in Id., *Opere*, Boringhieri, Torino 1979, vol. XI, 495-535.

Frith, Ch., *Inventare la mente. Come il cervello crea la nostra vita mentale*, Cortina, Milano 2009.

Godin, A., *Psicologia delle esperienze religiose*, Queriniana, Brescia 1993.

Green, Th., *Quando il pozzo si prosciuga*, CVX, Roma 1991.

Gregorio Magno, S., *Omelie sui Vangeli*, Città Nuova, Roma 1994.

_____, *Omelie su Ezechiele*, Città Nuova, Roma 1992,.

Heschel, A., *Il sabato*, Garzanti, Milano 1999.

Ignazio di Loyola, s., *Esercizi spirituali*, Edizioni Paoline, Cinisello Balsamo [Mi] 1988.

_____, *Autobiografia*, TEA, Milano 1992.

Ionata, P., «I guai del perfezionismo religioso», in *Città Nuova* 2 (1990) 44-45.

Johnson-Laird, P., *How We Reason*, Oxford University Press, New York 2006.

Kiely, B., *Maturità del ragionamento morale e maturità della vocazione cristiana*, in L. Rulla (ed.), *Antropologia della vocazione cristiana. III Aspetti interpersonali*, EDB, Bologna 1997, 157-225.

_____, *Il bene e la sua valutazione*, Manoscritto 1999.

Kolvenbach, P.H., *Folli per Cristo. La sapienza di Maestro Ignazio*, Borla, Roma 1999.

Lewis, C.S., *L'abolizione dell'uomo*, Jaca Book, Milano 1979.

B. Lonergan, *Il metodo in teologia*, Queriniana, Brescia 1975.

Manenti, A., *Vivere gli ideali. Fra paura e desiderio/1*, EDB, Bologna 1988.

Marcel, G., *Être et avoir*, Aubier, Paris 1935.

Martini, C.M., *Cattedra dei non credenti*, Rusconi, Milano 1992.

Martini, G., *Ermeneutica e narrazione*, Boringhieri, Torino 1998.

Melchiorre, V., *L'immaginazione simbolica*, Il Mulino, Bologna 1972.

_____, *Metacritica dell'eros*, Vita e Pensiero, Milano 1977.

_____, «Immaginazione», in *Enciclopedia filosofica*, Bompiani, Milano 2006, vol. VI, 5534-5539.

Merleau-Ponty, M., *Il visibile e l'invisibile*, Bompiani, Milano 1969.

Nietzsche, F., *Carteggio Nietzsche-Burckhardt*, Boringhieri, Torino 1961.

Perniola, M., *Del sentire cattolico. La forma culturale di una religione universale*, Il Mulino, Bologna 2001.

Paglia, V., *La via dell'amore*, San Paolo, Cinisello Balsamo [Mi] 2007.

Pascal, B., *Pensieri, opuscoli, lettere*, Milano, Rusconi 1978.

Pieper, J., *The Four Cardinal Virtues: prudence, justice, fortitude, temperance*, University of Notre Dame Press, Notre Dame, Ind. 1966.

Pontificia Opera per le Vocazioni Ecclesiastiche, *Nuove vocazioni per una nuova Europa*, 8 dicembre 1997.

Rizzuto, A., *La nascita del Dio vivente. Studio psicoanalitico*, Borla, Roma 1994.

_____, «Capacità di credere. Considerazioni psicologiche sulla funzione del credere nello sviluppo personale e religioso», 2007 (manoscritto).

Singer, Ch., *Del buon uso delle crisi*, Servitium, Sotto il Monte 2006.

Stein, E., *Psicologia e scienze dello spirito. Contributi per una fondazione filosofica*, Città Nuova, Roma 1996.

Spadaro, A., *Abitare nella possibilità*, Jaca Book, Milano 2008.

Tilliette, X., *Filosofi di fronte a Cristo*, Queriniana, Brescia 1991.

Tommaso d'Aquino s., *Summa Theologiae*, Edizioni Paoline, Cinisello Balsamo [Mi] 1975.

Yalom, I., *Guarire d'amore. I casi esemplari di un grande psicoterapeuta*, Rizzoli, Milano 1990.

ABOUT THE AUTHOR

Fr. Giovanni CUCCI, S.J. is an Italian Jesuit, with a degree in philosophy from the Catholic University of Milan. After his theological studies in Naples, Fr. Cucci obtained a masters in psychology and a doctorate in philosophy from the Pontifical Gregorian University in Rome, a subject he currently teaches in the same University. Presently, he is also a member of the college of writers of *La Civiltà Cattolica*.

Fr. Cucci's publications include *La forza dalla debolezza*, Adp, 2018[3], (translated and published in Spanish and Polish); *Esperienza religiosa e psicologia*, Ldc, 2017[2]; *Insegnare agli ignoranti*, Cittadella, 2016; *Internet e cultura*, Àncora, 2016; *Paradiso virtuale o Infer.net?* Àncora, 2015, (published in Italian, Hungarian, and French); *Dipendenza sessuale online*, Àncora, 2015; *Consigliare i dubbiosi*, Emi, 2015 (published in Italian, Spanish and Portuguese); *Church and the abuse of minors*, Gujarat, Gujarat Sahitya Prakash, 2013 (with Hans Zollner); *I vizi capitali*, Adp, 2012[2](published in Italian and Polish); *Il sapore della vita: la dimensione corporea dell'esperienza spirituale*, 2009 (published in Italian, Spanish and with this publication also in English).

Made in the USA
San Bernardino, CA
21 May 2018